Echoes of Youth

Stories of

reflection, discovery, and freedom

D. Shubert & E. Miller

To the person I once was

and have yet to become.

Echoes of Youth

On a cool September night, from a lonely maple tree on the quiet edge of summer's pardoning, parts a single leaf from its home in the sky that slowly dances upon the wind, catching the gaze of two young men in the street, as it falls to their feet. Alone in this new world, the leaf marks the start of something, the brink of autumn. The heat waves had passed, and the summer was coming to a close. That Friday night in September was one of Daniel and Elliot's last shots at a valuable summer memory. That night, September second, 2022, is the start of their story today. The night began at the house of a friend. There was a good group of people, but it wasn't quite a party. There were some close friends and some who seemed like they were there just for the alcohol. As the night progressed, they engaged in some casual drinking games, and everyone was beginning to get tipsy. After some antics on the trampoline, and some sitting in the corner waiting to leave, they were picked up by their friend. After a night of Truly's and White Claws, some fast food was much needed. McDonalds was the obvious option. Sitting in the parking lot, they were enjoying their greasy meals, and coming down off the alcohol. It's hard to place a finger on the inspiration for this, but out of nowhere, Danny seemed to have a revelation. He turned to Elliot and the words, "We should write a book" exclaimed out of his half-drunken mouth. Now this idea is something you would've heard before. A night of drinking and aimless conversation usually led to unreasonable ideas such as this. However, for some reason this idea stuck, and whether Danny said this with serious intention or not, an impractical yet alluring yet was planted in their heads. Danny's statement was initially dismissed by the crowd of friends who saw it as just another intoxicated scheme. But Danny and Elliot were motivated in that moment. Following the food break, they headed to their friend's house to crash for the night. It was rather late, maybe 2 or 3 A.M. by the time they arrived. Everyone was ready to get some shut-eye, except for Danny and Elliot. They stayed up to spitball some ideas about the book. Considering that they kept drinking, and it was 3 A.M., these ideas were rubbish and got them nowhere. After that night they hit a rough hiatus of an occasional mention of the book, but no real progress. See, the notion was always there. Write a book that presents their youthful experiences, to both recollect moments from their pasts, and to reflect on their experiences in the future. Months went by, and only a few brief references to the book crossed their minds. Danny was always more on board than Elliot, and it took some convincing for Elliot to go through with it. But one night in April, it suddenly hit Elliot the value that writing this book could produce, not only for them as the authors but for anyone who cared to read it. So they got to work. Before you continue reading, you must understand the purpose of this piece. This isn't just a documentation of the experiences of their lives, but they are attempting to dive into the deeper themes and perceptions that have impacted them thus far, and the ones to come.

The Purpose

When trying to pin down the purpose of this book, we realized there was not one main message or idea we are attempting to convey. Instead, the goal of this book is to serve as a sort of journal that will hold our thoughts and memories of our youth as well as attempt to describe the universal experiences and feelings of being a teen. The way it is often hard to remember what it felt like when we were a kid, we know that once we are adults we will likely forget what it felt like to be a teen. By documenting and reflecting on our life experiences we hope to grasp and hold a piece of that beauty of life within these pages. Along with writing this book to be inspired by our lives, we hope to leave a lasting impact on you, reading this right now. We hope you can reflect on your own lives and gain useful insight from us. We hope if you are someone older, that this book will reignite the memories from your youth and the nostalgia that comes with it. If all you take away from this book is some fun and memorable stories, our goal is equally accomplished. This book is for everyone to read. Our friends, our families, anyone we know, and even anyone we don't know, anyone can take away something from this book. Approach the following pages with an open mind. Be willing to reflect on your own life with the experiences of ours, and be willing to find as much or as little in anything we've written. Be willing to ask yourself any questions that might come up when reading, and be willing to answer any questions that arise from our writing. Now with all that out of the way, you are ready to begin reading.

The Drive Home from Camano Island

Daniel Shubert

I find the end of summer to have a very similar feeling year after year. It's bittersweet. It's moving. It's ambivalent. While I reflect on the nostalgia of the past couple of months, memories from countless years past are also awakened, stirred from a place within. Not only do I reminisce on the recent memories I had just made, but I feel those old memories brought back to me. Forgotten memories from my childhood are clear again and I remember those feelings I had as a kid. My family used to visit Camano Island for a large portion of July where we would rent the same house year after year. The house was on a stretch of vacation homes with beaches of driftwood logs and rocky pebbles in front. From practically my birth until I was around 10 or 11, I would spend every July at that house. When I look back at it now it may have been the happiest days of my childhood. The beauty of the

Pacific Northwest was at its peak in the middle of these hot summers, and my birthday on July 18th falls right in the middle of July and the summer as a whole. I have always been and still am a "Summer Person". I love the sun, hot weather, and the freedom of nature. When I was a kid all I wanted to do was explore the outdoors. I find happiness and freedom in the warm summer months, and as a kid, it was my favorite place on earth. I spent the month swimming in the cool waters of the Puget Sound, biking on back roads through quiet neighborhoods, playing games with my brother, sisters, and cousins. Everything a kid could want: fishing, fireworks, boating, birthday cake, green fields, warm pancakes, knee scrapes, dirty hands, tanned skin. But every year the same thing would happen. When it was time to leave the house and say goodbye to Camano, we would pack our bags into my dad's truck or mom's minivan and head on home. As the car pulled out of the driveway of that magical summer home, the thought of next year's summer was already looming in my childhood fantasy. Maybe my memory isn't perfect but it feels like almost every time we left that house I would see the most perfect sunset go down as we drove. As I sat in the backseat, looking out my window at the red and orange colors in the sky, I felt the most distinct feeling. A combination of emotions that is so difficult to put into words. I was struck with the joy sparked from what I just experienced in that month of pure childhood fun, but those feelings mixed with the sad thought of going home, back to reality. I can remember the way it felt so vividly because it's the same emotions I am experiencing right now as the summer of 2022 comes to an end. This feeling always seems to come back as the cycle of time continues, and each time it hits harder as I realize I am growing older. And when I watch a sunset fall at the end of summer, the red and orange colors that illuminate the sky bring me right back to the seat of my parents' car. Watching the sun fall and not ready to go home.

The Ledge on the Water

Daniel Shubert

A couple of days ago in May of 2023, I was feeling a bit down. Nothing really specific had caused this feeling, but more likely a combination of feelings and emotions that led me here. Maybe it was the uncertainty of my relationship with a certain girl, or the feeling of loneliness on a sunny day when you have no one to spend it with, or my constant confusion about where my life was going, or the many things I do when I drink too much. Anyway for all of these reasons and more, I was feeling a little down on that day. When the day seems cloudy, my thoughts are dull, and the world just seems a little dim, it's hard to know how to get out of that rut. Sitting around in my room would only leave me alone feeling worse. So I try many different things to make me feel better and lift my mood a bit, but none of them really work. The answer is quite simple, and it's been here all along. I needed to get out, near some trees and water where the air is clear and understanding. Going outside would clear my mind and pull my spirit out of the dark, so I grabbed my guitar and keys and got in my car. I knew exactly where I was going to go as I drove down the hill facing the water and the evening sun. Parking my car on a gravel patch on the side of the road, I walked to a small path hidden between some trees. Walking down the path, the sunlight shone through the late spring leaves and turned them a vibrant shade of green. I stepped in some muddy dirt but didn't care about keeping my shoes clean, the way you just didn't care about that sort of thing as a kid. The trail went on for a few minutes and ended at a railroad that stretched across the coastline. The forest and path I had come from stood behind me towards the east. I looked straight out to the water of the Puget Sound towards the west. The water was smooth as glass, and on it was the reflection of the infinite sky above. Across the water was the silhouette of Whidbey Island and to the left was the faint sight of the Olympic mountains off in the distance. The railroad was built on a large rock ledge that was built to separate the ocean from the forest and keep the railroad supported. This spot existed when I was younger and I came here many times as a kid. In my younger summers, my friends and I used to ride our bikes around town, to the store to grab snacks, and then come to the railroad to sit, eat, and laugh. Our legs used to dangle over the high ridge, and we'd spend hours just talking at that spot. We'd wait for the trains to come and watch as they roared past us with a gust of wind. The salty ocean scent filled the summer's air, and cool breezes made the heat bearable. So I found myself here again only this time my friends were nowhere to be seen. I sat down on the ledge, picked up my guitar, and began to play. If somebody else were to have found me sitting there on that ledge I would have looked extremely alone, but I didn't feel alone. I felt like someone was with me, or maybe I was just truly with myself. I felt comfortable in my presence and that inner lonely feeling began to fade away. You could sit here for hours and watch the sun slowly sink behind the island to the west, so that's exactly what I did. There's a specific thought I remember having, and it was how sometimes instead of watching the sunset it's more interesting to watch how the light hits everything else. I watched how the light hit the trees and reflected off the water. I let my mind drift and left behind the fog of thoughts that had been clouding my mind all day. This spot allowed me to get away from that constant rush of life that plagues our everyday. Eventually, the sun faded away, and the dusk crawled its way over the trees. When the sun dropped below the horizon, I packed my guitar up and made my way through the trail back to my car. The tranquil state that nature had brought me began to fade away, and the real world seeped its way back into my thoughts. There is no escaping the inevitable stress of life. Of course, you can get away and find peace of mind, but the world will always be waiting for you to return. The ledge by the water stood alone in the dark after I left. In its solitude, the stars came out and beamed their light on the calm water. The ledge was never bothered by the same anxieties, stress, and fears that I had. It remained untouched at its place by the sea, constantly at peace, and waiting for me to return.

Double-Edged Blade

Elliot Miller

Nostalgia is a double-edged blade. Nostalgia performs a complicated waltz within the fabric of our own existence. It can bring a sense of beauty to our lives that we often find ourselves yearning for. It reveals the complex nature of our past and the beauty that we ourselves hold onto from the past. However, nostalgia carries with itself a somewhat bittersweet demeanor. While nostalgia is a thing that allows us to appreciate our past, it potentially could obscure the complications of our past as well. My somewhat nostalgic outlook on life makes my childhood seem better than it was, but it always brings me a sense of comfort, knowing that I had experiences in my childhood that are worth remembering. Certain places, people, movies and games, sports, songs, they all have a special place in my heart because of the power of nostalgia. This in a sense, gives me the satisfaction knowing that if I miss those things now, they must have been really special when I was a kid. Nostalgia brings a compelling form of romanticism into our lives that paints a picture over our past, allowing us to view our past through a brighter-colored lens. Things that may not have been significant to us in the moment, are suddenly intensified with significance, as if nostalgia places an enchanting charm on our memories. Nostalgia doesn't even just affect me from my childhood, even experiences from 2 to 3 years ago I find a sense of nostalgia for. For instance, I weirdly find myself nostalgic for the Covid era. There was some weird comfort in being isolated when everyone else was as well. Covid forced us to adapt and change, with no one to influence us but ourselves. Isn't it strange that a time in our lives that was mostly terrible, and everybody wished would end, I find a feeling of reminiscence in? See, in this example, nostalgia unearths a sort of hidden beauty to that time in my life. It sheds light onto moments or things that otherwise would have been overlooked at the time. However, this is what I mean when I say nostalgia is a double-edged blade. Nostalgia has the ability to take us out of the present moment if we aren't careful. If we are so infatuated with moments of our past, in a trance of nostalgia, of longing, then we are actively taking our minds from the present moment, and placing them in the past. It is essential to bring a mindful appreciation of the past, but recognizing that fixating on the past can blur our view of the present moment. Appreciating the present is one of the most powerful things we can do for our minds, and yet, nostalgia often blinds us from it. Time and time again I find myself yearning for the feeling that nostalgia brings to me. It's as if it whispers into my ear, ever so alluringly, "Remember how good you had it? Where did all that go?" But as I remind myself constantly, the thing about the past is that it already happened. There is nothing we can do to change the past, and we can't relive it again. I find that I completely ignore that fact when under nostalgia's trance. Nostalgia for me ebbs and flows in the course of my life. I don't really notice it until I do, and then it is truly prevalent. Most of the time, there isn't even really an exact thing that I'm nostalgic for. I wonder if I mistake my discomfort of the present with a longing for the past. But my point here isn't that nostalgia is some evil force that wants us to be depressed about our present and wish we were in the past again. It can act as a tool for us to be grateful for the past and the experiences we were so lucky to have, but it can also cultivate a path for us in the present. Do your best to remain anchored to the present. Remain one of the same with yourself, in this moment now, even amidst the seemingly unstoppable tide of nostalgia. Every moment is a fleeting one. The time we spend reminiscing on moments of our past is time wasted on the present. Most importantly, remember this. The experiences of the present moment will too, one day, transform into an artifact of nostalgia. Isn't that comforting? To know that one day, we will all look back and have an immense appreciation for the life we live now? I call on to each of you reading right now, find wisdom in the threshold between the past and present, and dance with all that creates those abundant memories of yours.

The Move to Snohomish

Elliot Miller

I used to live in Bothell. I was born in Bothell and I was raised there until I was around 10. I had a cozy, comfortable house and I lived with my brother and parents. This house is where I credit all my childhood memories to. I had so many friends in the neighborhood, even one right next door. I remember tip-toeing my head over the fence to try to catch him in the backyard and ask for a sleepover when we had just had sleepovers the 2 nights before. My elementary school was right up the street, and the field where I used to play soccer was a 3-minute drive away. That neighborhood was everything to me. So many days were spent playing football in the front yard, swinging on the swing set in the backyard, and biking around to each of my friends' houses in the neighborhood. So you can imagine that when my family told me we were moving, it destroyed me. I remember the second I heard the news, I broke down crying at the dinner table while my parents were celebrating in the other room. They tried their best to comfort me and assure me it was for the better, but I wanted nothing more than to stay in that house. When we finally got settled into our new house in Edmonds, I was still depressed about the house in Bothell. I remember being a stubborn little kid, not allowing my parents to see one bit of happiness from me. I was set on showing them that I was devastated by the move. But as so many crying nights passed, and the days went on, I started to warm up to the house. It was way closer to all my friends at my new school. Edmonds is such a pretty area, and I grew accustomed to everything the area had to offer. There was Hickman Park right down the road, Sherwood Elementary across the street, and so many mornings, evenings, and nights were spent at Richmond Beach. I have so much nostalgia and love for my house in Bothell, but I think my house in Edmonds was more impactful. I really started to become myself in that house. But once again, pretty recently this time, I was met with terrible news that we were moving. This time to Snohomish. A 50-minute drive at best, and much longer with traffic. This news didn't come out of nowhere, however. My family, mom especially, had been looking at houses in Snohomish for close to 2 years. I never understood what the appeal was to them. I mean just to get to our house you have to drive 10 minutes in an isolated, remote forest. It really is nothing but forest, farms, rednecks, and the smell of cow shit. I dealt with the move to Snohomish better than the move to Edmonds. But what really killed me was the move to my new school. I moved schools at the same time I moved to Snohomish, and that was in October of 2022. The move may have always been in the back of my parents' minds, but this truly was a quick move for me. From the middle of September to the end of October, we had sold the house and completely moved. The idea to move schools came from my mom, and she did not give me much of a choice. So I moved schools. I never really connected with anyone at the school while I'm writing this while still going to this school, I realize I only really like a very small amount of people there. I was less depressed about this move, but I still wasn't on board with it whatsoever. I mean I really couldn't understand why my parents would decide to leave everything behind and move that far away. I let my mom have my word a few times about my dissatisfaction. But just like the move to Edmonds, it got better over time. One thing that truly saves me from boredom in Snohomish is the fact that one of my closest friends lives a mere 8 minutes away. The chances of that are so slim, that both of us would live up here, so far from everywhere else. We began to explore the area around our houses and came to find some truly remarkable spots, some of which deserve an entry of their own. I now realize that the nature here is unmatched. At nearly constant times during the day, you can hear some sort of wildlife. Our trail camera picks up footage of bobcats, cougars, coyotes, and the sorts. There are families of deer that seem unbothered by people, as they scurry through the neighborhood with not a care in the world. And at night, the amount of stars visible is more than I could ever see in Bothell or Edmonds. I found that once I got over the fact that I was so isolated from most people, it truly was such a peaceful place to live. It's nice to get out of the city and be in your own remote neighborhood, surrounded by nature. Writing this now, I don't fully love it here yet, but everything will come with time. I guess the point here is that when a circumstance feels pretty shitty, there is always a silver lining. We need change to grow as people, and each of my moves brought me that opportunity. Although it seems unfair, I am grateful for the move to Snohomish. I want to remind anyone reading this that gratitude can go a long way when we are unhappy with something. So if you find yourself in a situation like mine, be patient, and learn to accept it. I promise it will turn out better than it seems.

Panther Lake

Elliot Miller

In Snohomish, where I live, there are a series of lakes named 3 lakes. Now these lakes are pretty small, and the smallest of the lakes is named Panther Lake. My previously mentioned friend Brid, who also lives in Snohomish, introduced me to this lake. The idea came up one day when we were at his house pretty bored, and not doing much. He suggested we go and play fetch with his dog. Because it is Snohomish, and we have nothing better to be doing, I was all for it. As my Honda Accord tried its hardest to make it through the rough terrain and enter the boat launch, my curiosity grew. After a short, bumpy ride, We arrived. The only public entrance to this lake is through a small boat launch on a rocky, gravel road. As soon as we got there, and the yellow tint of the sun illuminated the tree line and the water, I realized that this lake was truly beautiful. It was surrounded by trees on all sides, and if you were just driving by the area, you would have no clue the lake was there. A few days prior to this visit, I made a spontaneous decision to delete all my social media. A few of my friends had done it, and I felt that I was on it too much, so I deleted it all. I have always struggled with feeling present in my experiences, my mind always tends to wander off someplace else. But arriving at this lake, I felt very present. The beautiful view and the wilderness atmosphere were all that was on my mind. And it felt good. For once in a long time. I felt the worries of life melt off me. This lake helped me to appreciate the area I live in more. The past few months I have lived in Snohomish, it has kind of felt like life just took a pause. Like I wasn't moving towards anything anymore. But I think I've mistaken the feeling of peace with that feeling. Snohomish, and all the beautiful parts of it, are as peaceful as it can get. I find that visiting this lake, I am at peace. This feeling is amplified whenever I visit the lake with my girlfriend. Someone who I truly feel safe with, combined with this magical setting, peace is the only thing that I can describe the feeling as. One day we jumped in the lake, and it was warmer than we expected. We found that the water felt so nice on our bodies, as we dunked our heads under, over and over, continuing to swim. After we got out and dried ourselves off, we laid down on the back of my car, with the spoiler supporting our legs. We had a few twisted teas to accompany us on our visit, and we just lay there. I remember looking up at the sky, it being kissed by the orange rays of the sun. I remember just appreciating that moment, appreciating her, and appreciating the lake. Now, as I go back and visit this lake, I am reminded of the special experiences that come to me in Snohomish.

Chelan

Elliot Miller

Every summer I try to make it to Lake Chelan. I'm sure Chelan doesn't need an introduction, but it deserves one anyways. Chelan is in somewhat Eastern Washington, and it is a 55-mile-long lake. The go-to place to stay is in the town, also named Chelan, and the towns surrounding it on the coast of the lake. Chelan is truly a wonderful place. The only thing to dislike about Chelan is the drive, but with the right weather, the right people, and the right soundtrack, it can turn a 4-hour drive into a seemingly short one. Now in Chelan, there are a few main places where most people stay. There is the lookout, just up the road from Chelan, there are a few miscellaneous condos here and there, Manson, Wapatao, and the main resort, Campbells. There are so many moments in my mind that I can recall in Chelan that are so dear to me, but one in particular stands out to me. This story takes place at the lookout. My recollection of the story is a little foggy, as it was a couple of summers ago, but me and my friends got on the road and headed to stay at the lookout. We chilled for a few days, not doing much. Then one day we went out and rented some jet skis. After hours of exhausting, but exhilarating fun, we got back to the house on the lookout. It was about dinner time, so we cooked up some Frank's Red Hot-style chicken wings, with some buttered corn on the cob to complement them. We had a challenge to see who could eat the most out of 40 wings, and I barely beat out my friends with 17 wings. After this, it was pretty dark out, and we had the idea to go to the pool in the neighborhood and have a late-night swim. The pool was of course closed at these hours but that could never have stopped us. Scaling the short, easily climbable fence, we were greeted with an empty outdoor pool, all to ourselves. The pool was a little bit frigid, and we weren't out there to be cold, so we chose the hot tub instead. Borrowing the pool inflatables, we floated around, face up, in the hot tub with the cool summer sky as the only thing in our sights, and nothing on our minds. But unexpectedly, I caught something in the corner of my eye in the sky. It was the moon. I don't appreciate the moon nearly as much as the sun, but on rare occasions, it's like the moon has something to boast about. The moon is a humble creation, but when it wants to, it can be the most beautiful thing in the sky. On this particular night, the moon was a bright, golden orb. I remember it being so clear, and with no clouds in sight, it was alone in the night sky, leaving all of our appreciation to go to the moon. It shone majestically over the lake, glimmering the water with a touch of gratefulness, as the water illuminated what the moon could not reach on the ground. After seeing the moon, I was blown away. It was like at that moment, I couldn't lay eyes on anything else so great. Just being in the already amazing atmosphere of Chelan, accompanied by the night sky and the rising moon, I felt as if I was meant to see this. With Parachutes by Coldplay as the album choice on the portable speaker, I imagined myself to be in a movie. This is the best I can describe Chelan to anyone who hasn't visited. It seems that no matter what the occasion is, you can always feel like the star of your very own movie in Chelan. Each and every summer I look forward to making the trip so much, sometimes more than once. Writing this in early June, as summer is approaching, I can only wait so much more to be back there again.

The Summer I Learned to Live

Daniel Shubert

When I look at my life up to this point, certain moments completely changed me into the person I am. When time slowed, and moments lasted forever. And when I think about them now, the nostalgia brings a beautiful melancholy. One of the most significant moments would have to be the summer of 2020. From the hot days of early June to the sultry August nights I saw myself live through experiences that would mark a turning point in my adolescence. I turned 15 in the middle of July and as the last reminiscent of any childhood innocence was slowly fading away, my eyes were bright with every new day. I saw myself discovering new music, wearing different clothes, and changing my attitude and behaviors. As the doors of this new world were opening, I was ready to charge into it with the force of my youth. Now this is also the year that COVID-19 hit, and with every day I was kept inside, I longed more to go out and live. As the isolation set in, my loneliness grew greater by the day. However, a trip to Decatur Island with my best friend Caden would change that, and would completely change my life for the years to come. Now I always went to Decatur for the fourth of July with Caden, but this year he decided to bring a group of his friends. I immediately felt welcomed by them, and it was one of those friendships that just seemed to happen so easily. And when you are that age there are no doubts. You meet someone, the connection forms, and before you know it you are calling each other friends. I found my spot in the group like I was always meant to be there. On that trip to Decatur, I developed a unique connection to each one of them. These friendships came to me at a time when I deeply needed them, and although they were new, I felt like I was home when I was with them. That trip marked the beginning of 3 friendships that would last for many more years. Later on, in early August I went to Lake Chelan with my family. Now I have been going to Chelan every year with my family, but this year my new friends happen to be going at the same time as me. We would both be staying at Wapato Point, a gated resort area that had several condos and vacation homes. It was a magical place where for my entire childhood I spent countless summer weeks enjoying the shivering lake water while the scorching summer sun beat down. My family rented a house, and my friends were staying in a condo. This specific trip to Chelan holds a special place in my heart and today I recognize how beautiful of a time it was for me. As I was learning what it was like to be a teenager, I spent a week with my family and friends in one of the most beautiful places in Washington. We spent days out in the hot sun and by the cool beaches of the lake. We swam, played games on the beach, jumped off bridges and cliffs, got whipped off inner tubes, and did flips off the dock that we thought was just about the coolest thing you could do. After dinner with my family, I remember being eager to go out and spend time with my friends. The jitters of excitement would fill me as I looked out the window into the promise of the summer night. My parents would be a little upset that I was staying out so late with them when it was supposed to be a family vacation. However, there is something so beautiful about going out at night under the bright august stars that never leaves my memory. Hanging around the resort at night was always packed with memorable experiences that were often the highlight of the trips for me. When we went out we always seemed to find kids our age to hang with. The friends you meet on vacation are always sort of a special thing. Since you know the friendship is just a temporary thing, there's a greater significance and meaningfulness with every moment. There are so many distinct memories and feelings that I can only attribute to my nights in Chelan. One night we lay in a grassy field and all looked up at the magnificent array of stars that wasn't quite visible back in western Washington. And as I breathed in the air, the sight of the stars reminded me of a subtle truth I often forget; I am alive. Every night we would make our way to the one hot tub on the resort, and meet whatever interesting individuals were waiting for us there. Our sunburned skin sizzled in the bubbling water, but our conversations never ran dry. On this specific trip, I even met a girl one night that I would develop a fling with for the remainder of the trip. Our fleeting relationship made the August nights even more dreamlike. I remember on one of the nights we went for a night swim with our large group of friends. We jumped into the cool black water, and reflections of the silver moonlight sprawled across the lake's ripples. As I treaded in the water, I looked around at the dark silhouettes of my new friends and although I couldn't see their faces, I remember the sound of their voices. Their sweet voices that, to this day, bring me comfort. The rolling hills that surrounded the lake were littered with houses. The warm yellow lights from the homes shined on us that night and I felt a boundless rush of what it meant to really be alive. My group of friends rushed out of the water and dried themselves with towels. They made it toward the beach and left me and the girl alone, so we got out of the water and sat on the dock over our laid-out towels. There was that awkward teenage distance that kept us apart. I remember looking out into the night trying to find the right words to say. Slowly the separation faded away as we struck up a conversation about just the most important thing to any 15-year-old kid, music. I now appreciate the simplicity of our conversation. How music could bring two people so close together because nothing else really mattered to me at that age. I know it mattered a lot to her too, or else she wouldn't have stayed there with me on that dock, and she especially wouldn't have let me lean in to kiss her. On that trip, I learned to see life differently. I looked at the stars in a way I had never seen before. I looked at the trees in a way I had never seen before. I looked at the water, grass, homes, and faces of my friends in a way I had never seen before. Learning to romanticize my life, I saw everything with a newfound beauty. I hope I never forget the way I felt on that trip because the feelings I had were surreal and something I had never experienced before. I'm not even sure if I've felt the same way since. I'm sure a lot of it had to do with my youthful naivety and longing to be out in the world, but there was a magical haze surrounding us on that trip. When I get older, I hope I don't forget the emotions that were felt that summer because I think as you live longer your mind just doesn't think the same way. Life just doesn't quite have that same magic it does when you are 15.

Alone in the Dark

Daniel Shubert

This entry begins like any memorable high school story, with a party. As I was revising this entry I decided to take out many of the specifics of people, place, and time as I'm not trying to emphasize the context of this instance. However, this night brought forth much reflection and left me pondering over its significance. For some basic explanation, I was at a party and felt relatively alone as I only knew one person there. Now the party began like any other, and as I quickly sipped down drink after drink, more unfamiliar faces entered the door of the house. Not wanting to be the guy standing in the corner, I made an effort to befriend the new strangers of the night. I introduced many of the people to new drinking games and tried to make friends with the other guys there. However, many of them were too high to remember the rules of the games let alone what my name was. With passing minutes, the party grew.

And in the quiet suburban house, a fuzzy atmosphere of vague faces and memories developed. For some reason, a bigger party feels much smaller and more personal than a small one. Because as the number of people increases, everyone forgets what is not right in front of them. My sense of attention began to be focused on a certain girl as the night went on. For the sake of her privacy, I'll call her by a fake name: Emily. Emily had pale milky white skin and a very apparent warm red blush on her cheeks. She wore a short white skirt that just covered her upper thighs and a light blue top. My pursuit of Emily honestly came as an inadvertent action probably driven by my intoxication and the fact that nobody wants to feel lonely at a party. After several instances of small talk conversation and exchanged moments of prolonged eye contact, we somehow made our way into the pantry of the kitchen that was hidden from the rest of the house. Many of the specifics become hazy when I try to remember how the night progressed, and differentiating who did what becomes difficult and frankly insignificant. However, we found ourselves in the pantry and the light switch switched off. We began making out in the dark and that distance that was between us in the party faded to nothing. Time moves differently when your mind is under the influence. It gets slow and speeds up at its own will, with no regard for the world. However, we soon recognized we had overstayed our time in the pantry and others would notice our absence if we were gone too long. She returned to her group of friends, and I waited a little while before leaving the room myself. It's funny how during a party you often totally forget where other people are, and you become so fixated on the thing right in front of you. This is why everything feels so intimate and personal, trapped in that moment. Emily and I let the distance between us slowly come back and continued to enjoy the night with the other people around us. It wouldn't last long though as a little while later we would find each other again in the upstairs bathroom alone. Again the light switch turned off and the dark room brought us together. We went on making out for a while then for some reason we dropped down to sit on the floor and her back rested against the wall. We sat there a while in that bathroom and seemed to care less if people noticed we were gone. Eventually, she suggested that we should probably return to the party, and I thought that she might've been worried that we would progress too much after only just meeting. I attempted to reassure her by telling her this was all we had to do, but we could go back downstairs if she wanted. There was hesitance over whether or not we should go back downstairs until suddenly I suggested for some reason that we could just lie there. Without a word, she understood what I said as she moved over top of me and we slowly sunk to lay on the floor. She lay on top of me, rested her head on my chest, and wrapped her arms around my body. I was surprised by her actions and the change of pace but gave in all together. I slowly reached around her and put a hand on her back and the other in her hair. Then we just laid. I felt the bitter touch of the cool bathroom floor as we lay down. The light weight of her body rested on mine. I slowly rubbed her back and felt the soft fabric of her shirt on my fingers. The room became quiet, and my mind raced with thoughts in the darkness. It was such a romantic instance for two people who had met in a rather unromantic way. Despite this, I felt a harsh distance between us, and this moment of comfort was truly a moment of desperation. I felt as though we were two lonely souls who had found each other for a night. We both wanted someone to hold and someone to make us feel less alone on that spring night, so we just laid there. I think a lot of people my age have felt a similar feeling. In a generation filled with hookups and temporary "romance", I think a lot of people feel a deeper loneliness and struggle to find meaningful connections with people. I myself tend to feel unsatisfied with one-night things, and yet I still find myself in situations where I seek out short-term "love" for that quick fix of intimacy and self-validation. So my body pressed together with Emily's to comfort the coldness in our hearts, and the night felt a little warmer just for the moment. I knew I wouldn't be seeing her again, and although I was fine with this realization my heart slowly sunk into a bitter isolation. I never felt so far away from her that night. I knew that in the morning I would be all alone again. I knew the warmth wouldn't last. I knew this wasn't love. How could I find love in a place like this?

The High School Experience

Daniel Shubert

The story of high school has been told again and again through many movies, books, and TV shows, and I think for good reason. High school is an interesting time and the experiences that happen in high school are often very sentimental and nostalgic for people. Although the typical stereotypes of high school may not always be accurate and movies like Dazed and Confused or The Breakfast Club are exaggerated, I still feel there is a very universal experience that comes with high school. High school in America is a timeless phenomenon that connects the youth across many generations. Yet I don't think high school is as great as it sometimes is portrayed, and I really hope I'll move on to much greater and happier things. To quote Randy "Pink" Floyd, "If I ever start referring to these as the best years of my life - remind me to kill myself." However, there is still beauty in the four years that are spent as you slowly prepare to enter the gates of adulthood. Some of the frivolous moments hold so much value to me. The glare of the lights, and the cool fall breeze of a football game in October. Or the empty fast food parking lots that you and your friends occupy for the night, illuminated by the warm yellow street light. These moments have not just been felt by me, but I'm sure you have felt them too, and I'm sure our parents have felt them and countless people from years past. Because these moments don't fade away. They are universal memories that are passed down from generation to generation. I always thought of the place I was raised as rather boring. The town of Mukilteo is a sleepy suburban town north of Seattle. It's quiet most of the time and almost entirely residential. However, this suburban American life is something I learned to appreciate. Although I don't know if I'll end up somewhere like this in the future. There is a distinct pattern to the way of life here, and it goes a little something like this: The high schoolers go to their Friday night football games where they play their rival schools, but nobody really cares about who wins except the players. Then after the games the players come off the field and talk to the other students and eventually somebody mentions a party. So groups of teens pack into their tight hot cars that their parents got them with music blasting. Driving through busy streets and quiet neighborhoods lit by street lights they soak in the life of their youth. Maybe stopping for a burger and fries on the way they eventually find themselves at the house party. They get out of their cars and carry in packs of beers and bottles of vodka. Music blares from speakers and voices shout across living rooms. Somebody will try to get in a fight while somebody else will try to get laid. And while one girl cries in the bathroom another is throwing up upstairs. Outside a group of people smoke their weed, and inside two reckless friends try to steal something from the house. The elderly couple across the street calls the police for a noise complaint, but the restless kids find a way to keep the night going. This continues for hours until eventually it dies down and the party falls asleep. In the morning the bright light wakes the hazy teens. Outside the sprinklers create little water droplets on the morning grass and the neighbor's mom walks her dog. Empty beer cans and chip crumbs litter the kitchen floor, and there is an unidentified stain in the living room. The house is quiet and the birds can be heard chirping through the cracked window. And next Friday the same thing will happen. And the Friday after that. For weeks, months, and years the pattern will continue. Those teens will grow old, create a life for themselves, and start a family on their own. Then their kids will become teens and do the exact same things. The cycle continues forever because nothing really changes. As generations grow old, the birds always chirp in the morning.

The Complications of Love

Elliot Miller

    I want to preface this entry by saying that I am not an expert on love whatsoever. I am fortunate enough to have experienced what I classify as love, specifically in a romantic sense. This entry is only meant as a place where I can write my experiences, perceptions, and complications regarding love. With that being said, I think it is important to do my best to define love. Love is a hard thing to define, as everyone's definitions are going to be a little bit different based on their experiences. The best way I can describe it is not being able to describe it. It isn't one specific thing that I can put my finger on. For me, it is a part of myself that is so deeply rooted in my soul, and my consciousness. I feel an outside force influencing it in every way, taking hold of it, and dragging it through a complicated mix of misery, happiness, loneliness, fulfillment, destruction, and pure bliss, all against my will.

Love is described as such a beautiful thing, but all of the unexpected side effects of love often go unnoticed. See, when you first fall in love, you are hit with a wave of pure happiness. It feels like your soul is permanently laughing, dancing around in the sun, hand in hand with the person whom you love. Everything is perfect. You and your lover are in another plane of existence, crossing the empty skies, all worries washed away by a wave of euphoria. You promise yourself, you're going to be the best you can for this person. You promise yourself, that you will never hurt them, that everything will be perfect. And for a while, it is. Each and every time you guys see each other, every worry, every problem you guys have disappears. Time ceases to exist. The feeling of a hug, arms wrapped tightly around their torso, or their back, that alone is enough to envision a whole life spent together, and it may feel like you two have already spent every past life together. Now, everything is perfect, everything is beautiful, but what happens next? Somewhere along the way, someone disappoints someone. Maybe you disappoint each other. An argument starts. The first one you've ever had. Bitter, hurtful things are said, and it feels like your world, your everything is ripped away from you. But oh well. You put aside your stubbornness and your ego, and you apologize. You make things right. Maybe it takes you a little longer than you'd wished. Maybe they are the ones who make things right. Either way, you two talk it out, you come to forgive each other, and everything is just back to the way it started. In some ways, it feels better than the start. You find that you have fallen in love, just a little bit more. But now you know the stakes. You know that things might not be perfect. And then, it happens. Often, you can't even pinpoint what it was. But *something* changed. And it changed for the worse. It feels like the love has been vacuumed out of your souls, and emptied into a state of decay, and darkness. You imagined a future together, you imagined living in a home, alone on a hill, with children, and everything was perfect. "Where did the love go?" "Why are we fighting every chance we get?" "Why is it that the person I love, more than anything, more than myself, is the person I seem to hurt the most," you ask yourself. If you haven't caught on yet, this "*you*" pronoun that I keep mentioning, is myself. This is my experience with love. And up to this point writing this, this is the state I'm in with my lover. I think of it as a snowball rolling down a hill. It keeps getting bigger, more and more "snow" sticking onto it, until it becomes so heavy that it can't bear the weight anymore. But eventually, the hill flattens, and the sun comes out. The snowball can stop worrying, it can stop bearing this weight, right? Until the wind picks up, the hill slopes down again, and the snow sticks more and more to the snowball, now almost a boulder. And it's like this keeps happening. It's a sickening cycle of healing and destruction. Fixing the problem, the love returning eventually, and it all being stripped away again. I'm sure anyone reading this can somewhat relate to what I have to say about love. There is so much more I could say about my experiences, but I want to cut it short a bit. The thing is, throughout all this hardship, all these feelings of inadequacy and failure, I find that love is the only thing I can rely on. When all else fails, my love for this person will never change. I might have a harder time showing it, but when I say I love you, I mean it. That is something that I won't take for granted. The ability to love. And although it might feel like we've hit a dead end, I will never stop loving. I think that is the only way it can get better. Throughout it all, every last sickening, sour feeling, if I can hold onto the love, then I know what I'm fighting for. I can't see into the future. I don't know what's going to happen next. I don't know what's going to happen with our future, but I hope if we both keep loving, one day, the bitterness will stop. And we'll experience *real* love. Not that honeymoon type of love, that real unconditional love, that won't fail. I've never experienced this feeling, so I don't even know if it exists. For all I know, it could be a myth. But I have faith. I have faith that it does exist, and I look forward to a time in the future when I know that I'm experiencing that. In the meantime, I'll just have to hold on for dear life, and I'll have to deal with it. But you know what? I can do that.

Sunset in Santorini

Daniel Shubert

I am very fortunate to have been able to go to Greece with my family for two weeks through late June and early August of 2023. We traveled around, visiting the many beaches, museums, historical sites, and towns that the country had to offer. Our third stop on this trip was the island of Santorini which is easily the most popular and recognizable island in Greece. It's known for its beautiful white buildings that stretch across the cliffs of the island. The main cities are tightly condensed with many buildings and tight walkways for the majority of the streets. From off the island, the awe-inspiring view of the white cities looks like snow atop the hills. Despite its natural and architectural beauty the biggest flaw with Santorini is how crowded it gets with tourists. In the daytime, you have to push yourself through tight crowded streets where sweaty tourists make their way around town through the stuffy heat. Huge cruise ships park in the island's caldera and shuttle boats let thousands of more tourists roam the streets for the day. There are few sandy beaches on the island which makes the go-to activity hanging around a pool or looking around the town. The natural landscape is truly a thing of wonder and fascination. The island itself is a volcano, and long ago it erupted and sank into the ocean leaving the cliffs poking out of the sea. The island is sharp, jagged, bare but all the same beautiful. From the city's cliffside walkways, the view is outstanding. The bright blue water stretches out to sea and surrounds various islands off the shore. Now there is a specific sentimental moment I recall. A magnificent occurrence that happened in Santorini, and was probably my favorite part of my time there. After a long day in the scorching heat, people go back home to take a shower, grab some food, and take a rest. Then when the temperature drops a good ten degrees or so the sun makes its way towards the horizon. The people come back out to the city wearing the nicest clothes. Girls put on their pretty sundresses and boys find their nicest button-up shirts. They make their way to the white ledges that rest along the cliffside walkways. Of course, they take their pictures and go on their phones, but also they slow down a bit. They put their phones away and take in the beauty of the sunset. I remember finding a spot on the ledge with my family. I sat on top of it and dangled my legs over the edge. Looking out to the west I saw the sun falling faster to the horizon and when the mist from the sea covered the sun it turned to a bright red circle. The sunlight reflected off the waves of the water turning it into a golden liquid of paradise. I couldn't help but romanticize the radiant atmosphere around me. Then I looked around me. I looked down the ledge to see the others watching this phenomenal event. Huge crowds of thousands of people packed the street doing the same thing as me. However, it didn't have the same rush as in the daytime. There was a peaceful tranquility that spread through the white ledges. All their eyes turned to the west and I saw the golden light reflect off their sun-kissed faces. I had been feeling rather lost in my life leading up to this event. I mean how could I not when I was a seventeen-year-old with no idea what I wanted to do with my life. I knew I didn't want to grow old working a job I hated, forcing myself into a lifestyle that did not satisfy me. I also knew that in a year I'd be getting ready to head to college which was just one step closer to the real world. So while I dreaded the potential unhappiness that came with the adult world, I also longed to explore it and see what it had to offer. Visiting Europe made me realize how big the world was, and how many different ways people chose to live their lives. There was an appealing fascination for the European world growing in my heart. It was different and new to me, and I wanted to see it all. I wanted to be a part of it, to live, and experience this different way of life. I could feel it in the air when I was there. The beauty, The magic. I knew I'd have to go back to the US and feel like I was missing out on some wonderful experience that seemed to be happening every day in the European summers. Maybe I was feeling lost. Maybe I had no idea what I was going to do with my life. Then I looked around at all the people crowding the ledges. I bet they all feel a little lost too. I bet we are all just people who constantly don't know where life is taking them, but hope that it works out all right. I looked down to my left a little ways where I saw a young couple in their twenties sitting on the ledge just like me. The girl was blonde with golden skin and very pretty. She rested her head on the shoulder of the guy who had dirty blonde hair that stuck out the back of his hat. Together they looked out to the sun and I saw the golden colors of love swirling around them. They looked like something out of a movie, and I believe they were very happy at that moment. At that same time a little boy, maybe 6 or 7 years old, bumped into me to my right. He was attempting to climb onto the ledge while his mother desperately tried to hold him back. Next to him was his brother, I'd assume, who looked almost identical in face and age. They held onto melting ice cream cones that had smeared all over their faces. One of them seemed to be taking in the view just like all the rest of us while the other seemed much more interested in the giant cruise ship down in the water. I can't exactly remember, but I think I recall their mother speaking to them in French. French was not the only language I could hear around me. I heard voices of Italian, Spanish, German, Greek, and much more that were unrecognizable to me. I picked up on conversations from Americans, Australians, and Brits. Around me were people from all over the world. I saw many faces of different colors, shapes, and ages, but they all were looking the same way; at the sun. I can't even begin to imagine the different stories these people had to offer. Where they came from. Where they were going. Who they knew. Who they loved. Who they longed to be. So I looked back to the sun and thought about my own life. What had led me here, where I was, and where I was going? Just maybe while I did this somebody else up the ledge was looking down at me, wondering just the same thing.

A Story of Separate Souls

Daniel Shubert

There once was a boy named Tito. He had tanned light brown skin, tight curly black hair, and an infectious smile. His good looks attracted people to him, and from an early age, he seemed to have his way with girls. Throughout his years in elementary school, he gathered many friends to laugh and play soccer with and always seemed to have another mysterious love letter waiting for him at his desk. Into his middle school years, his life didn't seem to change much, except now he cared a lot more about the girls. Tito also had a lust for the materialistic things of the world: jewelry, shoes, clothes, cars - they fascinated him. The stash of money in his bedside drawer would grow week by week until one-day society deemed that it was big enough and he would take it all out and head straight to the mall. Walking through the mall he peered through the glass windows and display sets at expensive necklaces and Jordan shoes. Eventually, something would garner his attention that he just so happened to have enough money for, so he would throw the wad of money on the counter, and just like that he walked out of the store feeling better about himself. However, after this, he did not decide to be content and go home. He would walk around the mall again making sure to show off whatever it was that he happened to buy. Walking past a group of girls their eyes would drift to him, and that made him feel good. There was a feeling that came with buying something new that made him feel good about himself. These things gave him power. These things gave him confidence. They gave him a greater lust to get just another thing, so when he made his way back home he again began to build that pile of cash next to his bed. This large affection for things of the wealthy world likely came from the fact his family did not have much money.

His parents were honest, hard-working people, but like a lot of hard work, there was little money to show for it. They had immigrated to the US illegally from Mexico in search of making more money and living somewhere where they could raise a family safely. Their life was very difficult, but they were determined and had faith in their futures.

Despite Tito's outward appearance, there was a sadness growing deep within him. When he was just a little boy his aunt, who was very close to their family, died. Tito used to go to her house all the time to escape any trouble at home or just for a spark of light on a dark day. She'd cook him delicious food and his cousins would be there to accompany him. He was always able to talk to her and she had a great way of listening and understanding him. Her death cut a wound in the boy, as well as the entire family, that would never seem to ever heal. The inner turmoil in Tito grew in the wake of his aunt's death, and with every day he grew older, so did his anxiety and depression. Nobody would have seen this on the outside, because every morning he put on a smile and walked through the world like nothing was wrong.

Once there was a boy named Dean. He was white but tan, had straight light brown hair, and soft understanding eyes. He grew up comfortably in upper-middle-class America. His parents raised him with little stress, and lots of love, and for the most part his days seemed to be bright and sunny. Dean was smart, he always had a way of figuring things out and making a good understanding of them. He was curious and often got himself interested in new subjects and hobbies. However, his intelligence did not prevent him from being a social and spontaneous person as well. He was smart enough to understand that not all things in life required constant thought and contemplation. When Dean entered his middle school years he did find some loneliness as he entered a new environment, but as time passed and he grew more comfortable he met somebody that would turn out to be one of his best friends.

Tito and Dean became friends in the seventh grade. Dean admired the way Tito seemed to attract people to him and gained the attention of anybody he graced with his presence. Tito appreciated the way Dean could listen and understand him. Despite Dean's suburban upbringing, the boys bonded over their love of rap music. Not just the mainstream stuff that everybody knew, but also the underground stuff that Dean had discovered and learned to love in his early adolescence. Tito introduced Dean to shoes, clothes, and jewelry and Dean began to find the addictive validation they provided. Dean's monthly allowance was now spent on shirts, jeans, and shoes at the mall with Tito where they both craved the attention that the materialistic items offered. Maybe much of this friendship was built on superficial things, but to the boys, it provided them with endless excitement. Then when the days came to an end, the boys crashed at one of their houses and would talk about the many things in their life. Their different pains, and struggles no matter how big or how small. Over time the friendship became more real. They told each other things they had never told before. With every day they grew older, they grew closer together. Although they came from very separate homes and families, their friendship became a rock in the stormy world of middle school. For almost 2 years they spent countless days exploring their hometowns, hanging with girls, playing sports, and talking about the insignificant wonders of being a teen. No matter what they happened to be doing they found a way to make it an experience.

Eventually, the friendship began to fade. Dean went to a high school with the rest of his neighbors from his town while Tito would be stuck in a lower class area. The physical separation slowly brought them apart. Tito's anxiety and depression would grow greater too, and he

became more isolated and lonely. The boys had reached a fork in the road, yet neither of them had a choice of which way they would go. Dean was destined from his beginning to take the high path, while Tito was cursed to lose his way. There was no stopping the extreme differences between the two, and although they both loved the friendship they had, they realized that their worlds were changing. They did not say anything to each other, but instead just slowly saw the other fade away. Tito went on to hang around a different crowd of people. The type of people that someone from Dean's part of town might describe as the "wrong crowd". His future held pain, suffering, and death. If Dean had known then what would come, he may have tried harder to keep him close. Yet Dean found other friends who were good to him and came from families more similar to his. The two never seemed to have cared about their separate lives when they were becoming friends, but that separation might just have been the very thing that brought them apart. Time went on and they never spoke again.
Sometimes Dean would wonder what Tito was up to. If he was okay. If he was happy. However, he never found the ability to reach out and catch up. And so the boys grew old, in completely different worlds, never to speak again. Their

friendship was frozen in time in a place they both would never forget.

The Innocence of Summer

Elliot Miller

Envision this, blazing heat reigns down from the sun above; sticky ice cream runs down your chin; And the sound of seagulls and waves occupy your ears, while the sharp, tangy aroma of the ocean fills your nose. What other time of the year do you imagine yourself in this paradise than summer? Summer is a unique time of the year. Summer is a time of reverie and relaxation. But why does summer hold such significance in our imaginations? Any other time of the year, we are occupied with school, extracurricular activities, sports, jobs, and whatever else may be thrown our way during the school year. As students, most of our time is spent fulfilling our societal expectations, often violating our well-being. Due to this hectic lifestyle, an awful lot of stress is brought upon us, leaving us little room to prioritize our mental well-being. But there is a silver lining to the calendar year as we all know, a literal ray of sunshine, a 3 month exemption from the rules that offers respite from the norm. Of course, I'm referring to summer. During summer, we are experiencing the most pure, whole versions of ourselves. We are allowed to shed the versions of ourselves that are burdened with the role of a student, allowing us to explore our true, authentic selves and desires. The freedom of summer is unmatched, a unique emotional state that we don't get the chance to experience during the school year. Each day is the start of a new story for us, allowing us as many resets as we want. The summer air is charged with ambition, and it gives us purpose. So many romantic flings, with the unwritten summer rule of no commitment; countless evenings spent at the beach, sipping on a few drinks, gathering around a bonfire with your closest friends as the smoke from the fire stains your clothes with its smell, providing a sense of togetherness, and carefreeness; and enough parties to give you a hangover for a week. Now of course there is more to Summer than women, parties, and substances, but what other time of the year could you get such an abundance, with no real worries of retribution? Summer is innocent and we are the innocence of summer. As I'm writing this, almost approaching a month of summer, I am happy to look back on what I have achieved and experienced, and I'm anticipating many more summer memories to come my way.

The Milky Way

Elliot Miller

A couple of days ago I joined my friends on a trip to one of their cabins. The cabin was located in Easton, Washington, a small and quaint little country town. It was placed on a nice plot of land, in a forested but dusty area, just off the freeway. And when I say dusty, that's an understatement. It felt like everywhere I looked, clouds of dust were forming in the air around me. These dust attacks were amplified when we took out the side-by-side, a sort of off-road terrain vehicle that got us around to our destinations in Easton. Our trouble-making friend, Jakob, who would lead in front of us in his four-wheeler, would purposely try to blast us with a dust trail every chance he got. The invasive cloud of dust and smoke would burn our eyes as we passed through it in our side-by-side, and even worse, it would find its way into our mouths and nostrils.

Our teeth would be stained with dirt, and our snot appeared black as we attempted to get it all out of our noses. Among swimming in a beautiful mountain-surrounded lake, and diving off a bridge into a frigid river, we found ourselves simply enjoying the nature we were surrounded by. We even had a little buddy join us while we played some drinking games on the patio. The goodest boy, one of the neighbor's dogs, came strutting over with a big rock in his mouth and tail wagging exponentially as he got closer, and we invited him over. The little guy wouldn't leave his best friend, his rock, no matter how hard we tried to take it from him. For reasons beyond my comprehension, he just liked having a rock in his mouth, and a pretty good-sized one at that. Maybe it kept his mouth cool, or maybe it kept him company. We took him inside, as one of ours, and gave him a nice big bowl of water. He gently set his rock down next to the bowl and went to town on the water. He then cautiously took his rock in his mouth again and followed us outside to watch us play our game. I kept him company while it was my turn out of the game. After he felt he was satisfied enough, he went and peed on some flowers, and began his journey back to his house, without a care in the world. Now our little buddy would be my favorite moment of the trip, but we had the opportunity to witness something incredible later that night. After a bountiful feast of steak and mac and cheese prepared by our friend Johnny, and a competitive poker game, we went outside onto the top balcony overlooking the property. Now at first, we didn't even notice it. A few of us were a few hits deep off of a weed pen, and others a few shots down. We went out there to enjoy a nighttime smoke, passing the goods around the bunch. Then, someone pointed out the stars. At first, I didn't think they were anything special, as Snohomish, where I live, has pretty low light pollution, so I was used to seeing more stars than most people. But as we lay our heads down on the balcony floor, and gaze into the night sky above us, everything begins to come into focus. The longer I looked, the more stars seemed to appear, and the more of the universe I could understand. Slightly coming into view, was a sort of white void visible behind the stars, I had trouble making out what it was until my eyes focused more, and I realized it was the galaxy, our galaxy. The Milky Way. It occurred to me that this was the first time I had ever been able to see the universe this clear, including the Milky Way. It seemed to paint with its own magnificent paintbrush and add a canvas for the stars to reside. It was so breathtakingly beautiful. It made me reflect on my life, and how much there is that I just haven't been able to see, or experience. It made me realize the significance of the universe, and the insignificance of my earthly problems. It made me understand how much more there is to the skies and the stars that watch over us at night. It was like we were looking at our own personal art exhibition, the universe the artist, the galaxy the art. We witnessed multiple shooting stars and a few unidentifiable lights and patterns that were intriguing. After this experience, I vow to travel to a place in the world where I can see all the stars and the whole beautiful canvas created for us in the night sky. I want to see it all.

The Puppet Analogy

Daniel Shubert

I want you to imagine yourself as a puppet: create an image in your head of a doll-like figure that vaguely resembles you. However, imagine it without any strings attached. Just a puppet floating around in a blank spot of space and time. This is how we enter the world. When you're young, you float around the world, unburdened by the weight and stress of life. As a child, you possess the spectacular ability to view the world through innocent eyes, seeing every moment as an adventure waiting to unfold. As you grow older, strings begin to attach to your puppet. Strings above the puppet pull on its limbs, taking away the unrestricted freedom it once had. The weight of the world attaches itself to you through responsibilities, reputation, stress, and countless other things that you didn't have as a child. These elements contort your puppet into uncomfortable positions.

This is challenging enough, but it becomes even more complicated when you realize that strings not only extend externally above your puppet but also connect from your puppet to the puppets of others. Your family, friends, lovers, and everyone you influence has a string connecting back to your puppet. So, while one arm of your puppet is connected to school or work, it is also connected to a friend or sibling. An interconnected web of all the puppets in your life, and everything becomes quite messy. Every action yields consequences. Everything you do, say or even think can affect those around you. A single moment can set off a domino effect through the strings of puppets, the outcome often uncertain.

When I started to realize this and became aware of my actions and their inevitable consequences, life grew significantly more complicated. As I age, it seems like more strings tug at my limbs, stretching and twisting me into unbearable positions. I grow tired from the constant pulling, looking for an escape. Now I want you to pause and observe the tangled mess of strings and puppets you're envisioning. Consider the pain and stress these strings cause the poor puppet. Examine the concepts they represent. Take a pair of giant scissors. And cut down those strings. Free the puppet.

This is how I felt during a road trip down the coast of Oregon and into Northern California. My cousin and I had a spontaneous decision to journey down the West Coast with a couple of used surfboards we purchased online and teach ourselves to surf. On a sunny July morning, we packed up the car with surfboards, sleeping bags, and backpacks of clothes, and embarked on a drive down Highway 101 that runs along the coastline. With no predetermined place to sleep, no set destination, and little knowledge of good surf spots, we set out to escape our lives for four days.

I noticed how clear my mind became during the scenic coastal drive and while in the chilly waves of the Pacific Northwest. Normal stresses and thoughts vanished. My puppet felt free once more, roaming the earth without restraint. The fact that we embarked on this trip without a concrete plan bred a slight sense of fear and uncertainty, but also an incredible feeling of freedom—exactly how life should be. Humans aren't designed for constant comfort. It's in our DNA to seek adventure and challenge ourselves in uncomfortable situations that remind us of what it means to be alive.

One evening, we drove to a beach to witness the sunset. After desperately searching for a place to sleep that night, we found a small campsite situated on a beach near the California-Oregon border. Arriving just as the sun descended, we rushed toward the water to capture the final moments. The sky turned pink, casting a magnificent aura of beauty over the vast expanse of sand along the coast. A radiance of colors expanded across the horizon like an explosion of life. Soft sand under my feet, the seagulls swirling around a massive rock, waves crashing on the shore, kids playing in the sand, a lone man walking the beach's edge—everything was present. And I was present too. I heard the sounds of the universe, the most glorious song. I breathed in the salty air, looked out toward the water, and sunk into that moment. Without any strings attached, simply floating in a blank spot of space and time.

Being Alone

Daniel Shubert

If you were to ask somebody whether I was an introvert or extrovert, you would get very different answers depending on the person you asked, the season of the year, the time of day, and whatever the most recent movie I watched was. I drift between the sides of the spectrum. Although I enjoy going out and love the attention and atmosphere of a social setting, I also love my time to myself. My mind is a place I constantly get lost in whether it's for better or worse, and I could keep myself occupied with my thoughts for many hours. When I'm alone I become very detached from my surroundings, and a world of its forms inside my head. This contributes to my creativity, and my constant drive to put something out into the world, but can also lead my mind into states of disassociation and loneliness. Being alone can be the best thing for you, but also it can tear you apart. In the moments

I spend alone, I can truly find myself. I can discover the inner workings of my mind and soul, but it can also go in the other direction. I can bring myself down with that little voice in my head. Ripping apart my ego, self-worth, and image. Like anything else in life, you learn that it is all about balance. To find that special state of happiness, I have to reach a perfect harmony in my inner peace with myself and feel connected to the people around me. I recently read a book that dove into many of the themes and ideas of being alone and self-discovery. While reading it, and then later watching the movie based on the book, there was a specific quote that stuck with me. The quote was short, simple, and yet so insightful, so here it is, "Happiness only real when shared." If this sounds familiar, it is because it's from Christopher McCandless whose life story was told in the book and movie *Into the Wild*. While nearing the brink of death of his idealist spontaneous life on the road, he jotted down this poetic phrase. At first, this made much sense to me, the memories you share with those special people in life are often the most memorable and captivating. Years down the line you can reminisce with your friends and family saying "Hey, do you remember that time…" And you have proof that that happiness and joy were real because it wasn't just remembered by you but also by somebody else. Almost like you now have proof that that happiness happened. Then I started to think about it a little more, and don't get me wrong, I loved the story of Christopher McCandless, and maybe if I was reaching my demise I would also have that same thought. However, at this current moment, I would have to say I disagree with Chris. Now Chris, don't get mad at me up there in heaven, but I just think you were wrong. This past year I've been doing a lot more things on my own. Things I would normally do with friends, I'm now trying to get myself to go out and seek that part of life on my own. Whether it's going out for food, shopping, watching the sunset, or exploring somewhere new, I'm learning to do it on my own. When I do this, I often find myself in a serene state of happiness. Sure, sometimes those feelings are accompanied by isolation and loneliness, but in a weird way that only amplifies my joy.

    Once I was swimming in a lake. It was just me in the water, nobody else was swimming. I heard faint sounds of laughter and shouting from the shore, but around me it was quiet. I slowly floated aimlessly around as my hands churned through the calm water. The evening sun rested at an angle in the light blue sky. Reflected beams of light skipped across the surface like stones and struck me in my eyes. I paid extra attention to the sparkle they created on the water. A type of attention that only exists when you're alone. Sinking deeper into the water, I submerged the lower half of my face. Just below my eyes, the water came up over my nose. I turned around in a slow 360 motion and took in the scenery around me. I really just took everything in and let whatever thoughts or feelings I had, come and go as they pleased. When my eyes reached the shore again, I saw her. She was waving to me with a big smile on her face. I liked her, and she liked me too, but right then we were separated. She could've swam with me, but she didn't and that's okay. Then I heard a shout a little bit away from her. It was my friends laughing as they played a game on the grass. I could've got out of the water and joined her, or joined my friends in their game, but instead, I swam back around. I turned on my back in the water, puffed out my chest, and allowed myself to float calmly in the breeze. I closed my eyes and came back to myself. I became aware of the way the water felt around me, and as I did this I became aware of another feeling I had. My heart became warm and as simple as this, I was happy.

So if you're telling me, Chris, that those feelings weren't real then I call bullshit. I'm not even sure he truly believed what he was writing. While Chris was out venturing the United States, and wilderness on his own, I believe that isolated happiness he felt was truer than anything else on earth. The very fact he experiences it alone makes it more beautiful. When you are alone, you can be more represented. Maybe I won't be able to reminisce on some of those moments of happiness with somebody else, and maybe my recollection of them will completely fade from my memory, never to be thought of again. However, that doesn't take away from the fact that they happened. At that moment, in that special place of time, I was there. I was existing, and I was happy. That's something nobody can touch, nobody can take away from me.

To Holden

Daniel Shubert

I was 16; in my sophomore year of high school. My year had started so well. I had been going out with a girl for a couple of months, had multiple groups of friends, was doing well in school, and most of all I was living in the moment. I was embracing my second year of high school with everything that it presented to me. I wasn't trying to live through an idealized expectation, but instead connecting to the realness around me. Fall is a beautiful time of year, and I spent it enjoying football games, high school parties, and with the people closest to me. Then things started to change. The chilled fall breeze that brought me life and excitement soon shifted into the harsh winter winds that I dreaded. On a night leading up to Christmas, during our break off from school, a friend of mine hosted a party. I drank slightly at that party, and as an odd atmosphere grew in the room, I asked the girl if I could talk to her outside. Thinking back now I don't remember why I decided to. When her gentle eyes began to shed tears, I remember wondering if I even knew what I was doing. Maybe it was the slight presence of alcohol or just a bad mistake. She had always treated me with kindness and affection, and for some reason, I was throwing that away. Outside the house, I told her I didn't want to be seeing her anymore, and that I needed to be alone for a little. After a final hug and a goodbye, she raced to get her friends and leave. I stayed for a while with my friends to talk about what had just happened. Following this, the days grew shorter, and the nighttime seemed to last forever. I became quieter; more reserved. Retreating into my inner despair, I became detached from the world. I wasn't seeing my friends as often and spent more time by myself. My days became an endless cycle of recurring events that brought me little joy, but I continued to do so. I trudged through the weeks with baggy eyes and a diminishing optimism. Becoming disassociated with the daily patterns of my life, my ghost walked through the halls looking for a way out. Every day it was the same. I woke up, my room was cold and everything outside my bed seemed so uninviting. I drove to school shivering and tired, with a black sky that represented little of the morning. I sat through classes as the harsh fluorescent lights were the closest thing to the sun that I saw. After school, I saw short glimpses of sunlight, before returning inside to a dusty gym for basketball practice. My body, tired and deprived of real energy made its way through this exercise until eventually it was over and I could go outside. When I opened the exit doors of my school's gym, I was disappointed to see that the sun was already fading away, so I returned home. After a shower, I'd sit on my phone, scrolling mindlessly until I'd eat dinner. After dinner, it was much of the same, with an occasional moment of doing my homework. Then I'd slowly make my way to sleep and prepare to do it again tomorrow. There were little moments when my mind felt clear anymore. My loneliness grew, and that rush of life in my veins dwindled.

Then something came to me, out of the blue. I was searching through a pile of things in my garage, looking for a book that could serve as a healthier alternative to scrolling on my phone. Then out of the rummage, like the rummage in my mind, came a copy of J.D. Salinger's "The Catcher in the Rye". The cover was torn, but I examined the image of a horse that I was able to make out. I had heard of this book before; how it had been regarded as a classic. I decided to give it a shot and took it up to my messy bed to read. I don't want to give away anything of this book if you haven't read it before, because I recommend that you do. However, it is a story of isolation and loneliness, and it struck me at a time I needed. I connected deeply to the protagonist, Holden Caulfield, who represented the angst and isolation of a teen in distress. He was a greatly flawed, unreasonable, and sometimes irritating character, but so was I. I was far from perfect and hated the way I was seeing the world with such sadness. The personal voice of the novel, and first-person perspective, made me feel as if Holden was talking to me. He told me of all the sadness he saw in the world and told me that I wasn't alone. He was there with me in my sorrow. I never knew I could find so much comfort in a work of fiction, let alone a novel. On those cold winter nights, something as simple as a book brought me comfort and warmth. I wasn't a reader before I read The Catcher in the Rye, and now I consider myself a somewhat regular reader. It made me realize the power a work of fiction could have. Whether it's a novel, movie, or story of some other kind, they can connect with you and give you comfort. If you ever have felt alone, or maybe you are feeling it right now, just know it can get better. It'll take effort, and you have to be willing to make a change. However, Holden, you showed me I wasn't alone. To the reader, I hope you have someone or something that shows you that you are not alone either. Somebody somewhere has felt the same way you felt or are feeling now, and they made it out alright, so you can too.

The Girl in the Tiger Tee

Daniel Shubert

The thing I remember most about her was the tiger on her shirt. Of course, I still remember her ocean eyes, sandy hair, and perfect upturned nose, but the graphic print of a tiger on her light pink shirt will never fade from my memory. She told me it was her favorite animal, and when I pointed to the turtle pendant on my chain, I told her this was mine. I can perfectly recollect the image of her wearing the shirt. How once she stood so close to me and made me feel like I had a chance. She stood with a grace, and elegance that persuaded every man to desire a piece of her perfection. I was not any different. In my eyes, she was irresistibly flawless. Every imperfection went right over my head as the energy I felt from her was pure. She was undoubtedly beautiful, yet different. Something made her stand out from other girls. Every moment I spent with her carved a unique place in my memory. Although my time with her was unwillingly short, it for some reason felt so profound.

I met her at a college football game in the transition period from late summer to early fall. We were both starting our junior year of high school, but she had come to the game with her friends, and I was working at one of the concession stands. I remember I was wearing a hoodie underneath my oversized work polo since the night sky brought a cool air with it, a sign of the nearing autumn. Early in the second quarter of the game, while I was busy filling up sodas and handing out food, she approached my stand with a bright bubbly smile. I was struck with awe at the way her radiant glow entranced me. Her friend adjacent to her ordered a Coke, so I filled up a cup and handed it over the counter. I told them to enjoy the game, we exchanged smiles, and just like that she was gone. I immediately glanced at my friends working next to me, and we all seemed to acknowledge how pretty she was. I got back to work taking orders, but her smile lingered in my mind. Some time passed in the game when eventually she came back to my stand again accompanied by her friend. This time it was she who ordered water. I took my chance to ask her how she thought the game was going, and made short small talk. I found out what her name was, and told her my own. Again I handed over the drink and she left with a smile. The side eye and laughter from my friends convinced me that her second visit was entirely intentional. I wished I had said something more, or asked for her number, but now she was gone. On the floor, I noticed a spilled cup next to my feet, so I bent down to clean it up. After wiping up the drink and tossing the cup away, I rose back up to the register, and there, just across the stand, was her face. For the third time, she stood in front of my station smiling and looking at me with her light blue eyes. It was just her this time, no friend. I greeted her, and she asked me for one last thing, my number. I spent the rest of my shift with a smirk on my face, and the thought of her in my head. She had already gotten a hold of me. At this moment I was already in too deep. No matter how hard I tried I just couldn't shake her, that's what she did to people. Later that night, once I had got home from the game, I texted her a little bit. We continued with some small conversations until eventually I drifted off soundly into my sleep.

    The girl in the tiger tee had a sort of class to her. She was well put together and gave off an aura of sophistication and poise. I would learn that she played golf, attended a private catholic school, and had been working a summer job as a lifeguard at a country club. Every action she made was calm and prudent. To me, and I think to most, she was the obvious example of a golden girl. Not only in her natural beauty but also in her character. From my impression of her, she was kind, and although her surface-level attractiveness was apparent, she had a realness to her. Her words didn't seem shallow or dull, and I sensed that if you could just break the ice off of her, a gem was awaiting inside. She never gave me the impression of being superficial or stuck up, but unintentionally she seemed to walk higher than the average person. In a crowd of people, she rose above the rest. She was special, unique, and if there is a god out there, he must've put extra time into her.

    The day following the football game where I met her, my friend was hosting a party. I decided to wishfully invite her even though we had only just met less than twenty-four hours before. To my complete and utter shock, she agreed. Leading up to that party, I don't think I had even been so nervous to see a girl. The truth was I wanted her. I wanted her bad. Not just to be with her or get closer to her, but I wanted her to like me. I wanted her to see something in me the way I saw everything in her. I know it might sound dramatic to be so infatuated with someone you barely met, but if you've ever met a girl of her sort, which is unlikely because they are so rare, you might understand. That night she and her friend came to the party. I greeted them outside the house and showed them the way in. It took me a bit by surprise when she introduced her friend who was named after a certain German luxury car brand. Once we were inside I showed them around the house a bit and showed them where they could get a drink if they wanted. This is when my eyes were drawn to her shirt with the tiger on it, and when she stood there I couldn't help but admire her presence. Most of the night went by like a dream. We stayed together almost all the time and struck up interesting, charming conversations. Her words told me she was special. That she had more to her. Going into it I thought that maybe she was just going to be another shallow pretty girl, but she wasn't. She told me things that seemed personal, and genuine. Our conversations only reeled me in closer, raising me higher and higher. Eventually, I'd have to fall.

We separated from the party and went swimming in my friend's pool alone. As wistful stars littered the sky above, the glow from the summer moon left an enchantment in the night. The pool water reflected the ripples of light on her face, and her eyes seemed to blend in seamlessly with the colors. Her wet hair was slicked back fully revealing her pretty face, and mine draped messily over my forehead. Looking into her eyes, I saw something. I don't know what it was, or even how to describe it. Staring into their depths it felt like sparkling white waves crashing on a lonely beach at night. I've never seen something like that again. Quietly, we drifted into the warm pool water and looked up at the beautiful stars in the sky. That's when I kissed her for the first time.

Sometimes I wish I had never had the chance to kiss her, and never had the chance to get so close. It wouldn't have hurt as bad when I realized I could never have her. We spent the rest of the night together, and she told me things even more personal about her. I opened up too and was taken off guard on how close we were getting. I learned of her fears and struggles, and I told her mine. She came to me so fast, in the blink of an eye. She opened up to me and showed me the beauty of who she was, but just as fast as she came to me, she disappeared. She went away in a blur, and suddenly I was awakened from my dream. I would only see her once more after that night. A brief and rather insignificant encounter, and then after that she faded away completely from me.

She was the girl of my dreams. If I were a young Gatsby, she was my Daisy. Her existence in my life was so short and temporary, and yet that only made it more pure. The thought of her rests deep in my mind, protected from the decay of time. She came from somewhere far finer than me, in both class and virtue. So far from me and out of reach, her perfection was greater than anything I was. Maybe I romanized that night. Maybe she wasn't the girl I imagined her to be, but the look in her eyes told me differently. The thing is, she wasn't just another pretty girl who thought she was better than others. I wouldn't be writing about her if that was the case. Her sweet disposition was something truly charming and special. Anytime she entered a room, something changed. Anyone who talked to her got lost in the sea of her eyes. I knew her future was bright, because anywhere she goes the sun is out and the birds are singing. That night lives in my memory but feels closer to a forgotten dream. Sometimes when I close my eyes I can still see the image of her tiger with a little green light in the sparkle of its eye.

The Ducklings Still Swim

Elliot Miller

This is somewhat of a hard entry to write, but I feel that it is necessary to my character. To set the scene, this situation happened a few weeks ago. I won't be getting into any details but all I'll say is that I had some complications at home. It was a really complicated situation that I had been at the tail end of. Looking back, maybe it wasn't the worst thing in the world, but on that day, it messed me up pretty bad mentally. I felt that I did not belong at home, so I left. I just walked, uncertain of where I was going, or what I was to do. Eventually, I asked if my friend could pick me up, and he did. So for the remainder of the night I just kind of went with him and we found things to do. Eventually, we settled at another friend's house to spend the night. I had been doing okay that whole evening, in terms of not thinking about what had happened earlier, but as soon as I lay down to go to sleep, It violated my every thought, and I realized at that moment that this was kind of a haunting situation. Eventually, I would fall asleep, and then wake up, and have to face the harsh reality of my day again. Unwillingly, I went home, but only because I had nowhere else to go and I had work later that evening. I wouldn't stay home for very long however, I didn't really have anything to do but anything was better than being there. So I decided to go swimming. It was a beautiful day, and very hot out, so I thought this would be the perfect thing to clear my mind. The lake of choice was Panther Lake, a short drive from my house. Upon arriving, I sparked up a joint, in an attempt to further drown out my feelings. And thankfully, the combination of exotic flower and the glimmering lake made for a perfect recipe for numbing the bad emotions, and bringing out the ones I cherish. As I made my way down to the water, I was excited, but anxious to go swimming by myself. I had never really done that before, So I didn't know what to expect. But entering the water, I found that it wasn't uncomfortable, it was inviting. As if welcoming me with warm, open arms in my time of vulnerability. I made my way further down the water until my head was completely submerged. Normally, the feeling of being completely underwater is somewhat daunting to me, but this time, I was met with complete serenity, as the tranquil water guided my swim. Upon returning up to the surface, I took in the land around me. I simply tread the water, looking around at everything before me. I am very familiar with this lake, and everything it has to provide, but this time, It felt as if it were my first time there. The sun seemed to shine just a little bit brighter, the water gleaming just a little bit more. The trees seemed to sway without a care in the world, and the water was the perfect combination of refreshing, but warm. And alas, as I made my full rotation looking around the lake at the nature around me, my gaze settled upon a group of ducklings, playing around in a bunch of lily pads. The water around them glistened, as if directing my gaze even more. The lily pads shone, not an ugly green that I usually perceive them as, but this time a perfect hue. I only wished I had my camera out on the water at this moment, to be able to capture this scene. Sadly, I didn't, so I had to use the next best thing, my eyes, to capture the moment. And in this moment of pure, unfiltered bliss, I was simply reminded that although I was in this moment of dread following everything that had happened to me in the past 24 hours, that life still existed.

Life was still beautiful, through and through. And I was grateful, not only that I was able to come across this happy, unbothered family of ducklings in my times of grief, but I was grateful too, that throughout all the anguish and troubles of the world, the ducklings still swim, and to me, that is beautiful.

Seventeen: The Threshold Between Childhood and Adulthood

Elliot Miller

To be seventeen years old is a weird feeling for me. I've pretty much escaped the freeing feeling of youthfulness, the ability to float through life without any real responsibilities or worries, yet it feels like I'm not old enough to make any significant difference as an adult. It feels as if I'm stuck in a limbo, not yet prepared for adulthood. As I reminisce on my recent teen years and even my years as a child, I feel very grateful that I got to experience that, but deeply saddened too, to know that adolescence is something that we only get to experience once and that we can never relive again. I look back on my younger self, who wished so badly he was older, mostly because I always assumed I would have more freedom. That is partly true now, seeing how my parents are much less strict about rules and such, but in a sense, I feel I had more freedom as a child. It felt like I was unbound to the hardships of life, as if life walked hand in hand with me, into whatever new experience I came across, cheering for me along the whole path. There were less worries of retribution, of consequences. And it was truly freeing. But in a sense, I could argue that the freedom I experienced then, is a different freedom than the kind I have now. At seventeen, I'm able to make a lot of decisions for myself, whereas back then, I needed more guidance. Maybe that's what I'm anxious about for adulthood. The pure excitement but also difficulties that come with making your own decisions. It is a weird feeling for me, this nervousness for adulthood, but at the same time, I find a sense of anticipation in that nervousness. I know that these are not the best years of my life, at least I would hope not. I would hope that I'm able to blossom, and carry myself into adulthood with upright confidence, and reap the benefits of independence. So while I am still seventeen, I suppose the best thing I can do is enjoy what little time I have left in my youth and anticipate an abundant adulthood.

The Miles I've Gone

Daniel Shubert

There is no greater turning point in one's adolescence than that special day you get your driver's license. For most, it happens on their sixteenth birthday, when it seems like they are finally entering the adult world and getting the freedoms that come with it. It's crazy how a little rectangular piece of plastic could provide someone with so much independence. The entire world seemed to be at my fingertips when I finally could drive wherever I wanted. Now that I am eighteen it's unbelievable to think that it's already been two years since I got my driver's license. But when I think back to how many memories I've made, so many of them involved driving. I mean I've probably had some of my happiest moments inside of a car. The countless number of nighttime drives with friends where the music is blasting and everyone is laughing. Maybe we were going somewhere or maybe we were just driving around for the fun of it. No matter what you happen to be doing, the drive is sometimes the best part. It's not always about where you are heading, but just that you are happy along the way. I know it's a common cliche, but it's true. If I'm with the people who love me most, or even just embracing the comfort of my solitude, a drive can make me appreciate the journey.

One of the reasons I love driving so much is for the music. Almost every vivid memory I have of driving is tied to a specific song. I remember driving home from a party on the 4th of July with two of my best friends when one of them showed me Bon Iver's "Holocene" for the first time. As we laughed about our night, the melancholy melody assured me how special of a moment it was. To this day it is one of my favorite songs, and it made me feel the magnificent feeling that summer could bring. Bon Iver seems to be a recurring motif in my life as I have another vivid memory of listening to his song "Lump Sum" when driving through a harsh snowy night. I was heading home on the highway by myself in December when a rough wave of snowfall began to dump from the sky. I was a little concerned if my front-wheel drive Acura sedan would make it home alright. However, when Bon Iver's mystical vocals flooded from my car's speakers, I saw the snowfall as a magical winter wonder. My Acura's headlights shined on the falling flakes of snow and they glistened in the black night. I felt the beauty of winter, and in my car, I trekked those lonely snowy roads all on my own. I can also remember countless days and nights of driving around with my best friend listening to our melancholic, slightly emo, rock music. When the summertime reached one of those lonely, boring sort of days, the best thing we could do was just drive around and bask in our moody adolescence underneath the small town streetlights. Or when I was driving towards the beach as a sunset filled the sky with colors, and suddenly "Pyro" by King of Leon came on. Then I turned to my friend, and the excitement lit up on both of our faces because we knew there was no better combination. The intro guitar riff transcended me into a summer daydream as I drove. Then right when the drop hit and the drums came in, I was instantly consumed by the music. The drive, the music, and everything else, it just all makes sense. It all just feels right. I wish there were better words to describe it, but I'm sure you have felt it before.

The Forgotten Moon

Daniel Shubert

It's September second again. Exactly one year since that day I planted the idea of a book into our heads. It's funny how things always seem to come back around. Sure time moves on, and every day I get older Yet in a way, time feels like it's just going in circles, like the wheels of a bike on a summer's ride. As this summer slowly comes to a halt, even though I'm a year older now it feels very close to how it felt twelve months ago. The first red and orange leaves have found their new home on the sidewalk, and the nighttime no longer has the balmy sense of the summer's warmth. No matter how much older I get, autumn will always be there to follow summer, and the cold winter air will always turn to the life of spring. The never-ending cycle of time that is the seasons is truly one of the greatest marvels this world has to offer. They connect so deeply to the human soul. With just a change in the weather, I always feel a profound change occurring within myself. The trees are tied to my spirit; the rivers to my mind; the mountains to my body; everything is one. But still, I am eighteen. I can feel the reality of adulthood creeping its way into my life. Sometimes I feel as though the thrill of youth that resides within me has to surrender to the normality of being mature. I know I'm still only 18, but I can't help but feel that as I get older my life is becoming more static. With growing responsibilities, it's hard not to think that maybe I was happier when I was just sixteen. Those days when the world seemed so new and exciting and all I wanted to do was run out into it with no care. Maybe I smiled and laughed more back then, and that's just the way life goes. However, just last night something happened that made me reject this idea. September first. No longer that magical month of August that's filled with sunsets, and days of intense heat. The night started with a high school football game, and packed cars full of excited teens awaiting their Friday night. I want to skip past all of this though, and talk about the end of the night. After a terrible blowout game that we were on the losing end of, and a pit stop at Dick's Drive-In for some burgers and shakes, the night was coming to a close. Now at this point,

I'm standing in the parking lot with some of my friends and the idea comes to jump in the lake. This is when the path splits. Anything in life can serve as a metaphor for something greater. You just have to be willing and thoughtful enough to find its meaning. So like the poem by Robert Frost: two roads diverged. The majority of my friends wanted to just call it a night and go back to the comfort of their homes, but a couple of them wanted to go night swimming in the lake. This is when I had a choice. I could follow the crowd and go back to the comfort of my bed, or I could make something happen and go for a swim. Maybe it's insignificant to compare this one decision to life as a whole, but maybe that's just what life is; a choice. And so I made mine. Two friends and I split from the group and made our way to the lake. The full moon watched over us, and lit up the water's surface. We walked through the dark shadows of the moonlit park, and out onto the dock stretching over the lake's surface. With little thought, I plunged into the silver water. Its warmth reminded me that my summer was not fully over, that the thrill of life was not yet gone. Floating in the September moonlight, I contemplated the thoughts that brought me to write this entry. And when I looked up at the full moon, it felt like I was seeing someone I once knew but had forgotten. Seeing it there in the late summer sky, I was reminded that this feeling doesn't have to disappear as long as I don't let it. Everything I do is a choice. Youth and spontaneity are not something that just fades away when you get older, but it's a choice to let it go. The silver rays rested atop the tranquil waters, and my mind was at peace. My life is just that. "My" life. It's up to me, and only me to make the decisions that turn my life into what it is. I only get to walk this earth once. I can try to live it like someone else, or try to do what everyone says will make me happy. However, what is more important to me is that I live it my way. As long as I'm willing to make a change in my future if I ever find myself unsatisfied, then I will be okay. No matter how old I get, no matter how many mistakes I make, no matter how many dreams I give up on, there is always a chance to make my life what I want.

Ode to a Fleeting Summer

Elliot Miller

September is here again, but I don't mind September. As much as everyone hates school, it's always a little bit exciting to start a new school year, even more so my senior year. My birthday is also in September so that adds some excitement. However, as I sit here in Septembers' embrace, I reflect on yet another summer that has come and gone. I wish I had gotten a little more out of this summer, but doesn't everyone wish that when it comes to an end? Regardless, it's evident to me that this year constituted a unique, but special summer. I find a deep appreciation of my experiences in these three sacred months, and I feel the need to share those experiences and feelings. Maybe it's a vain attempt to hold on to whatever's left of my summer fantasies, but I feel the need to share it. After all, that's what this book is all about. So without much of an introduction, here is an Ode to a Fleeting Summer.

It is June, and the beloved thrill of school's end is ever-present. Summer's warm open arms are slowly embracing me. The sun begins its journey on its fiery chariot, once again reigning over our sky. I feel it begin to elegantly kiss my skin on these early June nights, soon to grant me that tan glow that I look for in the cold winters. The air carries with it a newfound scent of blooming flowers, ever so alluring to my impatient mind. I imagine that Mother Nature saves her best fragrances for us to enjoy in the Summer months. The days begin to stretch out, carelessly, as if the calendar as I know it ceases to exist. As the bottom of my feet graze the meadows of this new warm utopia, I find myself welcoming summer's embrace, with nothing to leave behind, and everything to gain. The evenings begin to shift. I notice a new symphony of colors in the world. The fogginess brought on by cloudy winters and rainy springs begins to fade, and everything becomes clear to me. The starry night sky, the entrancing flow of the ocean waves, the dark green evergreen trees, everything becomes vibrant. It's as if Summer has taken away my doubts about the world, and offered me hope in the form of natural beauty. My June ends with a hike to a special kind of lake. A lake that dwells on your mind with excitement the whole hike up the mountain. A lake that makes the sweaty journey up the rocky, dirty terrain all worth it. A lake that lights up every part of your adventurous soul when it finally comes into view. Accompanied by someone close to me, we finally reach our destination, and our troubles melt away from us as we submerge into the clear, but freezing water. At first a daunting task, but one that adds the final bowtie on top of our journey through the mountain. Even though at this moment I have July to look forward to, For June, I am grateful.

It is July, and June has just surrendered itself to the second month in the trilogy of summer. That scent of blooming flowers in June has now metamorphosed into a full blossom in July. The world seems to urge me to discover, to adventure. Each day is a new page ripped out of a rose golden storybook. I find myself being called by the enchantment of water. The ocean, lakes, and rivers are all fair game for a soul-cleansing swim. My body ignores the glacial temperatures of the waters, and the sun rewards me for it. July is a month of freedom and the present moment. Between a beginning and end, July really is summer in all of its graceful glory. July is a movie with no bad endings. A movie that leaves you staring at your TV for minutes once it ends, begging for more. As I chase the sunny horizon, the wind rustles my hair and clothes, as if providing me with friendship in my hopeful chase. The canvas of night welcomes the brightest stars, all strung together with meaning, interpreted however is wished by those brave enough to decode their message. I visit the beach time and time again. The beach is now a haven for all who visit. The silver aura of the moon presents itself to the waves. Sand gets in my shoes and socks, but I don't mind. I take deep breaths, and oxygen becomes one with each breath. July brings with it the 4th, and too, come the fireworks. I recall laying up against my car with Zoe, overlooking Richmond Beach as our gaze darts back and forth at the horizon at whatever house lights up a firework. The deafening, but almost comforting booms shake our world as we celebrate together. Each boom we heard replicated each warm heartbeat of ours in that moment. My July ends with bittersweet memories. I can recall some tears, some happy, some not. I recall a feeling of dread, knowing that August is marching forth, and there's nothing to be done about it. But I also recall an immense appreciation for July, as I do each summer. As I wait for July to return next year, I have one month left to look forward to. For July, I am grateful.

It is August, and I begin to hear a bittersweet melody in my ears. For each day that grows shorter, my memories grow richer. I learned to cherish every day that I have left. August is a time of reflection on the past few months, yet one last chance to savor that sweet taste of summer before it fades away from me once again. August is a time of both relaxation and one last chance at adventure. August whispers to me, "Child, do not forget the seductive charm of summer. The seasons will change, and with that, so will you, but keep this moment treasured deep in your heart and soul, and it will find its way back to you." I picture myself in a hammock, tied between two trees rooted firmly in the field below, the wind singing me a quiet lullaby of comfort. I hear someone call my name in an urgent tone in the forest beyond. I look, and nothing is there. My name is shouted again, but no one is there calling it. It's at that moment I realize the calls of my name are from within, an attempt to reconvene the summer adventures I so desperately long for. My August ends in the countryside, with a special someone. We start the drive out east, in an attempt to escape the parasite that is light pollution. After about 30 minutes we pulled off the road into a patch of grass and weeds along the edge of a forest, overlooking acres of farmland. A red velvet blanket is laid out below us, and we ourselves lay down and look up into the ever-so-dim evening sky. As we wait for the stars to appear, we talk. We talk about nothing special or extraordinary, but we talk. Finally, the first star appears above us. Then another, and then another, until we are staring into the watercolor that is the night sky, full of the many white specks that are stars. I point out the constellations I know and make up ones that I don't. We discuss life and the mysteries behind it. We share our opinions and viewpoints, and we find meaning in each other's thoughts. And as I lay beneath the ever-expansive galaxy above me, I don't feel the usual despise I have for the ending of summer. At that moment, I feel ever so lucky to be, doing something I love, being able to appreciate the creations of life. In that moment, I didn't let the bittersweet melody of August tear me down. Instead, I feel it build me up. From deep within me, a place inaccessible in most cases, I feel an otherworldly shift. As if the spirit of these sunny days and bright nights itself has entered my soul, reminding me that it is never truly gone. Then, without a moment's notice, August is over, and with that, summer is too. As I write this with the dread of the first day of school waiting for me tomorrow morning, I am reminded that August is beautiful. August is independent, with its own sets of rules to follow and emotions to ponder. As I begin the journey to wait so very patiently for summer to meet me again on the horizon, I remind myself, for August, I am grateful. For summer, I am grateful.

The Urge to Disappear

Daniel Shubert & Elliot Miller

I often get the urge to disappear. Into the unknown, into a world I've yet to discover. To escape the things I run from, and at the same time, discover the things within myself. At night, when the world seems vacant and empty, I imagine a place far away. Where the birds are chirping and the stars are brighter than they are here. Maybe it's my young impressionable mind that skews my view about the life I currently live, but for some reason, I find discontent in the modern world and the societal expectations brought upon young men and women. The expectations to do good in school, graduate, Go to an even more sophisticated school for 4 or more years, get a degree, settle with a job that will likely make you want to kill yourself, and continue that life until I settle down and keep struggling to make ends meet. When I'm alone with my thoughts and my mind is clear, I imagine a life for myself. To live a life on the road where I don't measure my value off the things that I own or the money I have but by the moments I experience and the beauty in my everyday. I'd wake up somewhere I've never been and as I watch the sunrise over a mountain, I'd think about the wonderful joy that lies in my soul. While others crave the new shiny materialistic properties that validate who they are, I'd be content with where I am and the moment in front of me. With every new car, clothes, or expensive item comes a desire for more. A desire that never ends, but instead feeds the greed that lies within us. We are never satisfied by these worldly possessions, but we continue to suffer a never-ending urge. I want to escape this cycle and find something more. Something that reminds me I'm alive. I'm taken back to a story that I read about a man, Christopher McCandless, who I draw deep inspiration from in this passage. He urged me as a reader to rid myself of the comfort I was so desperately confined in. The point that comfort is the killer of man's spirit resonates so deeply within me. The hard part about writing this entry about the "urge to disappear" is that it is so easy to romanticize a life with such minimal responsibilities, a life on the road, running from nothing, but everything at the same time. It is much harder to follow through on that fantasy. The problem is that I am likely to just go down the path previously stated, the path that society expects of me. I can only hope that one day I wake up and everything I do and desperately desire in my life will hit me like a freight train, and my entire consciousness stream will shift into another realm. I envision, at the end of my life, staring death in its dark, sunken eyes, a flash that appears before me. If within that flash I see days gone by of sitting in traffic, working an unfulfilling job, and waiting for my life to come to me, I will be disappointed. Disappointed in myself for not becoming the person I longed to be, and letting my days pass. To not have seized the moments that I was given, I'd leave this world with sorrowed tears in my eyes. Yet if within that flash I see the world that I love, in all its glorious beauty, it will all have been worth it. The beauty I find in nights underneath the heavenly stars. The beauty that resides in snow-capped mountains and valleys of rivers flowing. The beauty in the faces of the people I love. The beauty that comes to me as I drive into the horizon as a setting sun paints my face with golden hues. The beauty I know exists in my coming future. I will greet it like an old friend, like someone I always knew. I may have felt lost, but I was trying to find something. And when I leave the world with a smile on my face, I will finally realize what I have found.

The Lonely Mountain

Daniel Shubert

Out there somewhere far away, there rests a mountain. In its place high up in the heavens it rests above the world and everything in it, looking down with utter peace. Completely undisturbed it watches the progress of time. It observes how the leaves of the forests bloom and perish through the cycle of the seasons. Every year it feels the bitter snowfall swallow its rocky ridges. It waits peacefully through the winter until eventually the clouds part and the sun frees the mountain from its snowy entrapment. It knows of the beauty that humans can create. Their culture, art, music, and rich history. The mountain can hear the faint whisper of the human songs drifting their way through the valleys. However, the mountain also knows of death. How the humans kill one another. How they lie, cheat, and steal. It sees it all, the perfect balance of good and evil. And at night, it embraces the silence of the world and watches the stars litter the sky in a place even higher than the mountain can reach. The mountain has been here forever. It observes everything. To the mountain, life does not have a beginning or end, but it is a cycle of forever.

I'm Daniel. I am just a man, but I often wish I was a mountain. I long to be as grand and wise as the mountains are. That's why I find myself so drawn to them. Atop the mountain, I find a feeling of understanding. There are endless names that these feelings have been called. The entirety of human existence has worked to define such peace through religion, art, and everything else. I can best put it into words as "when things just make sense." Whatever name one gives to it doesn't really matter, because when you feel it, you know. It's when your mind suddenly becomes tranquil. When the normal fuzziness of my thoughts seems to dissipate, all that remains is clarity. It's when I look around and realize that everything around me is connected. That I am just another piece to the puzzle that we call life.

It's the middle of August. One of those summer days when you have nothing to do, and nowhere to be. In my backpack, I throw in my camera, journal, water bottle, an apple, and a small bag of trail mix. I hop in my car and begin heading east, towards the mountains. As I drive, the suburban neighborhoods and cemented pavement gradually fade into evergreen trees and towering mountain ranges. Weaving through the valleys and hills, I reach a trail and begin my journey. The trail starts calm and steady, inviting me in. Surrounding me are boundless trees, trickling streams, and the soft murmur of birds and insects. It all reminds me of my childhood. For some reason I feel light, and weightless like I did as a kid. Mother nature reminds me of stories from my past, from summers long ago. I can feel the energy of those sunny July days of my youth radiated in the trees around me. A smile stretches across my face, and deep within my heart, it burns a familiar warmth. As the trail progresses and the sun reaches its peak above my head, the path becomes steeper. The joy remains, but the feat becomes more challenging. As I trudge on, the nature around me pushes me forward towards the top. At the end, the dirt trail turns to rock. My steps become large strides up steep boulders and stones. The mountain is giving me its hardest right before I reach the top. My mind is fixated on pushing through until I reach my destination. Just as my legs begin to give out, the path flattens and I see what I came here for. Before me is a bright blue lake surrounded by mountainous glacier cliffs. I take it all in and find a spot on a rock to rest. I observe the new world I have just entered. The wildflowers, the trees, the glacier lake, the steep rocky slopes, and the feeling in my soul. I jot down some notes in my journal and think about where I am. I would've stayed up by that lake forever if I could. I swim alone in the chilly mountain water, take some pictures, and enjoy my delicious apple. Packing up my stuff, I say one final goodbye to the lake and mountains. I begin my descent back to the real world, and on my face is a gift from the mountain; a smile.

On a Tuesday in early September, a day before I go back to school, I embark once again for a hike by myself. This time as my car makes its way to the trail, I notice that something is different. I drive through a long, bumpy gravel path that leads me deep into the forest, and when I reach the trailhead, the parking area is completely empty. This time I am truly alone. The whole area is deserted, and I feel so far away from everything. On the sign for the trailhead is a general bear safety sign, and although I know that bear sightings are rare, I can't help being scared of the possibility. Due to the fact that I was miles away from any civilization and that there probably hadn't been a single other soul on this trail today, the fear of a bear seized me. As I began my hike toward the peak, I kept thinking "What if". What if there *was* a bear? I was alone with nothing but my camera, journal, and some trail mix. Even if I tried to reason with a potential bear, I don't think bears like trail mix enough to prevent him from eating me. It went on for a while, and I couldn't shake the thought from my consciousness. Finally, I realized that what I was worried about was just an idea. Until an actual bear came out of the bushes and confronted me, there was no point in fearing something that did not exist. In life, we have a lot of these "bears". Ideas and fears form in our heads and hold us back from doing things. But what I realized at that moment was that there was no point in fearing something that was not right in front of me. Especially when that fear could be the very thing holding me back from reaching my peak. I continued, and with every step closer to the top, the bear faded away from my thoughts until eventually I reached the sky.

On the lonely mountain, everything makes sense. Perched on a smooth rock peak, my head seems to breach the edge of the sky. Soft clouds drift serenely in the lofty expanse above. Rolling hills of lush evergreen trees, and sharp cliffed ridges sprawl out for miles on end. One quiet town is visible from off in the distance, but from here it looks like a ghost town with no importance at all. In this place, way up in the mountain, time stretches, bends, and loops around itself. Feelings from long ago come back to me unexpectedly. I remember when I was little and spent summers running through sun-dappled forests, wading in cool creek waters, and riding my bike through silent streets. I remember driving with my friends at 16, and how the shine of the city lights made me feel infinite. I remember how she caught me with the look in her eyes as we lay out on the grass. I remember the songs that took me far far away. I remember it all. Although I am only just 18, I feel I have lived a life worth millions.

As I sat on that rock, a mirage of an old friend approached me from the dense underbrush. His face is warm and smiling, but within his innocent eyes is a singular golden tear. I ask him why he's sad, and for what reason is his unexpected visit. He tells me that he is going away forever and that he came to say goodbye to me one last time. His words burn slowly and resonate in a place deep within my heart. I ask why must he go away forever, why won't I ever see him again. He explains that there comes a time in every man's life when they must say goodbye to something they love. My eyes turn sad, but I understand what he means. I tell him that I love him and that I miss all the days we spent together. He explains that those days still exist, that the love is still real, but just that now they live in a memory. He comes closer to me and stretches out his hand. Reaching out, I shake his hand but say not a word. He turns away from me, and with his silent farewell, floats off into the clouds, dissolving into the world.

On the lonely mountain, I remember what it all means. At the edge of eighteen, with the quiet haze of beauty that the summer always brings, I leave my youth behind me. The beaming glow of the sun filters through the battered leaves and climbs the trunk of the towering evergreens. The shimmer of light catches my eye, and a gust of wind whirls through the heavens and everything beyond. I sit secluded in the presence of nature, and the thoughts from within myself. On the lonely mountain, as my gaze drifts far toward the horizon, I breathe and listen to the song of life.

Devastation, Yet Resurrection

Elliot Miller

It was a dim fall evening. The air was crisp, yet slightly nippy. I'm joining my close friends at a local restaurant, for a surprise birthday party for one of our good friends. We gathered at the dinner table eagerly waiting for his arrival. At long last, he comes strutting in, unaware of our presence. We loudly welcomed his arrival, we laughed, we ate, we celebrated. Soon after, we gathered at our friend's house to celebrate the rest of the night. After a while, me and my good friend Daniel Shubert, who some of you may know, decided to depart from the group and go out on a little quest. The series of events that followed are somewhat of a blur, but I recall us arriving at a gas station, friendlily talking to two homeless people, and then asking a hooker to buy us nicotine pouches. To our surprise, it worked. Not without a little bribery of course. We then ventured into the nearby Edmonds waterfront, expecting to be alone on the pier. However, the pier was filled with fishermen all the way down to the end. We went from one fisherman to the next, making lighthearted small talk. We came to learn that these men were fishing for squid, which happened to be in season, and were worth a pretty penny. We then settled on chatting with a group of two young fishermen, who had some funny stories to tell us. One of them claimed to be a sort of transcendental being. He said that everything we have experienced, and will experience, he has already lived through. That one stumped us quite a bit. On our way to leave the pier, I spotted a bucket of slimy, dead fish, unguarded by the man who owned it. Deviously, I crept up, grabbed a fish, and scurried off before he could see me. Me and Daniel snickered, because, who wouldn't in that moment? I then had the idea to throw him back into the water, because I really had no use for a half-dead, stinky fish. But the fish seemed to flutter around in my hand as if trying to swim through the air, an attempt to grasp the last bit of life he had in him. I tossed him far below into the cold black waters, and we patiently waited to see if he would swim off. A minute went by, and we saw no signs of life. Jokingly, we got down on our knees, looked up into the heavens, and prayed to God. We prayed that God would give this fish another chance at life, as we felt the fish didn't deserve to die. We said amen, and looked over the ledge at the fish. We waited, very patiently. At first, we thought our prayer had gone unanswered, as he was as still as could be, bobbing up and down on the surface of the ocean waves. All of a sudden, the fish's tail began to flutter, ever so slightly. Then followed the rest of his body. He began flopping around, before finally swimming off, away from our view. Me and Daniel were in awe. We looked at each other as if a miracle had just happened, and in a sense, it did. I thought this would be the most impactful moment of our night, but I was beyond wrong.

Arriving back at the car, we began our journey back to our commune of friends. We had the idea to play "Heroes" by David Bowie in an attempt to reconvene the echoes of our summer adventures. Anyone familiar with the song will know the emotions that it conjured up inside of us, and that a high-speed cinematic moment was necessary. I accelerated up a long stretch of road, pushing my foot down hard into the pedal, increasing the speed on the dash with every passing second of the song. We sang our hearts out, and let out a few whoops into the youthful night sky, enjoying the highlight of our night. Unbeknownst to me, my whole life would change in the coming seconds. As I looked ahead to the road in front of us, I noticed that our turn was coming up on us, and coming up fast. While I pulled Danny down from out of the sunroof, I watched as we came speeding up on the turn. One moment of lapsed judgment later, I veered into the turn thinking we could make it, when I realized how tight the turn was. Slamming onto the brakes, and attempting to veer the steering wheel away was no use. The moment that followed is almost burned into my head. I can see this one clear frame of a memory every time I think back on this night. Us in the car, staring dead silently ahead as we rapidly advance toward the guardrail. I can see the rail and the dark forest behind it. I can see the street lights above it, shining a chilling light down into us. I can see the street we were supposed to turn onto, just mere feet away from our reach. We proceeded to shoot violently, straight into the guardrail that awaited us. Time seemed to slow down drastically. A deafening bang, a rumbling shake, and a moment later, we lay in the ditch on the other side, smoke rising, airbags deployed. I was in complete and utter shock. I looked at Daniel, mouth wide open. I looked down at my hands and legs. I thought to myself, "Am I injured? Shit, am I even alive? Did that just fucking happen?" As the demolished frame of my car lay smoking in the ditch, my mind raced. How could I be so stupid? How could I wreck my car, and for what? Speeding down the road to a good song? As the minutes passed while we waited outside the car, wondering what to do, my disappointment in myself became increasingly burdening. I felt like a complete and utter fool, and rightfully so. How could I put my good friend, my fellow author, in that kind of danger? How could I put myself in that kind of danger? It truly was a devastating moment, one that I will never forget. But somehow, amidst the chaos and destruction that rested before me, I thought back to that moment on the peer. I remembered my prayer to God, about giving that fish a second chance, one that I thought he rightfully deserved. I drew an eye-opening parallel to my current situation. On the other side of that guardrail, was death. Complete and utter death. A death that would have been so quick for us that we wouldn't have had the chance to think twice about it. But that guardrail stopped us. God stopped us, and he was speaking to us at that moment. I could almost hear him say to us, "This world is fragile, just as quick as I have given you life, I can take it away." But just as that fish came to life and swam away, we walked away from the crash without any injuries, other than a few scratches. Everyone who later saw the scene of the crash was in complete awe that we were even alive. Despite how devastating this was to us, I was extremely grateful that we both were able to walk away unscathed.

Fast forward to the present day, the time of me writing this. These last few months have been extremely difficult for me. I find myself in a place in my life that I have not yet been to, true suffering. On top of the crash, my girlfriend and I parted ways after 8 months of being together. While it was probably going to happen sooner or later, it still hurt. Needless to say, I have been stuck in my house, and my head quite a bit, and my times alone are not always the brightest. But I don't want this to be a sob story. I want this to be a real story. A story for me to look back on and be able to say, I lived through that, and I am okay despite the trials and tribulations I went through. I am almost certain that when this whole stage passes by, I'm going to be a better man because of it. Even already, I can feel myself healing from these daunting challenges. Without a car, I have been alone a lot at my house in

Snohomish, far from my friends and school. Therefore, I have had a lot of opportunities to sit in silence and think. I have thought a lot about a whole lot of things, some bright, some dark. But to each of them I give credit to my crash because without it, I would not be able to be in this state of self-reflection. Some of those thoughts are as follows. Firstly, I want to get back into shape and eat healthier. I know I sound like your dad on New Year's Eve, but seriously, I want to do anything I can to better my mental health, and I think that's a good first step. I used to be in the gym a lot. In fact, it was probably the biggest priority in my life. However, that life has long passed me, and I feel disappointed about it. But I want to incorporate that back into my routine. I've been going on runs, doing pushups, and starting to include genuine, healthy food into my diet, so I feel I'm making okay progress there. I've also found myself being drawn to meditation and journaling a lot more, a form of self-reflection I find helpful. I find that it seriously helps me to control my negative and anxious thoughts, and remain present, something I have recently struggled with. But I still have some work to do to be able to consistently do those things. I've been doing a few more things here and there, and while I have a long way to go, I can feel my mental health getting better, and I'm proud of myself for that.

The thing that's been lingering on my mind, is how stuck I feel right now. I have a lot of goals and a lot of ambitions. And maybe they're all just fantasies, but I want the opportunity to make them as real as possible and I feel that I am very far away from that. Normally in these entries, I would have some sort of lesson or happy ending but currently, that's where I am right now, and I want to be as transparent as I can. That means accepting my vulnerabilities and sharing them. However, I'll leave you with this, and I hope you can see a part of yourself in my writing. While I look around and see people in this world, it baffles me how we have collectively settled on some of the priorities deemed important for society, by society. I then look at myself and reflect on what I find important, and what I want to succeed in, and it seems vastly different than the masses around me. But while we all worry about things, I seem to be worried about what I'm missing out on to fulfill myself. For a long time in my life, I've felt unfulfilled. Not in a depressing misunderstood way, but in the way that I think I could be doing more for myself, or that I'm doing the wrong thing. Ultimately, more days than not, I find myself yearning. Truly, yearning for something. Yearning for experience. At night when I close my eyes, I envision myself in the grand, snowy mountains, living off nothing but the subtleties of nature, and that which I find peace in. I envision myself in a distant foreign country, joining a community of people, who were birthed in a society so different from the one to which I am chained. I envision myself creating. Creating soul-capturing music, like those songs that you can feel deep in your chest, like it's poking and prodding at some hidden, buried emotion. I envision myself creating films, the type that makes you shed a tear as you watch, the type that makes you get up and pace around your room as if you had just been enlightened. I envision myself painting in a quaint, humble studio, giving every stroke of the brush a personal touch of detail. I envision myself capturing breath-taking pictures, and displaying them for all to marvel in. Most importantly, I envision myself experiencing. Not just existing in this world, but truly experiencing. I say this right now, in the hopes of holding myself to my ambitious promise. If in the next few years, I don't find myself fulfilled in whatever I'm doing in life, I'm going to make a drastic change in my life and make that happen. And I mean that, I can swear to it.

I know this entry was long and all over the place, but I promise it's all connected. I consider this to be my last, and most impactful entry in this book, so if you made it this far, I reach out to you with immense gratitude for taking the time to read it. I know I said that I wasn't going to end this entry with a happy ending, but I changed my mind. With one final word from me, I want you to soak this in as best you can. I recently heard a quote from a man named Chris Booth that goes, "The way to live your life is to do the things you want to do, not just the things you feel like you have to do. And then, do the things you want to do with absolute intensity and full focus. If you can do that, you'll be happy, and you'll be better." I think that quote perfectly encapsulates how I want to live my life. It always comforts me, knowing that people have a similar view on life as me and that I can find wisdom and guidance in their words. In the same way, I hope you can take away something meaningful from my words, as that is my biggest goal with this book. Thank you.

Echoes of Youth

There comes a time in life when everything must come to an end. Relationships, seasons, that cup of coffee that hits just right in the morning. In the same way, our story has now reached its end. Yet with every ending comes a new beginning. The same way the end of summer brings fall in its place, and you don't stop loving just because you lost a lover. So while our story today has come to an end, the never-ending storybook of our lives will continue to write its own boundless stories. As life moves forward, let our words serve as a reminder to everyone to let their own storybook be written by their life experiences. Every book requires a pen and paper. Let your experiences be the ink, and your mind the pages. Let your thoughts flow through the pages, good or bad, unfiltered. Throughout these pages, we have learned that every moment deserves reflection. To live without remembering is to have never lived at all. The complex properties of life; painted by the vignettes of memories and moments, songs, sorrows, trials, and tribulations, each is worth recognition. Without taking a moment to reflect on our pasts, we lose the purpose of it. We let our memories slip through our fingers, and dissipate into the sea of everything that is meaningless. But take our young impressionable thoughts with a grain of salt. We rather you go out and implement our callings into your life. Go for a walk. Swim in a lake or hike through those mountains. Listen to your favorite sad song and have a cry. Find those things in life that make you want to reflect. At the same time, like a river that diverges into two, be optimistic about everything that will come to you in the future. There are new adventures to be had in this world. New experiences to live through. The breaths we take now are the same ones taken by us in the past. So follow the path that leads your future, and remember the path from which you came. Those blank pages of your mind that seemingly never get filled, will one day be written in the stars. We hope that we can provide you with the tiniest bit of insight from what we have gained in this life so far. We hope that you take our stories in these pages, and go write your own.

On a cool September night, the idea for this book came to us. An unreasonable notion, but one that stuck with us. Almost exactly a year later, on a gloomy September afternoon by Mukilteo Bay, our dream has come full circle. A set of drunken words from two lost teenager's mouths come to fruition on this fateful day where we type the final words of our story. We reflect on everything we've accomplished with 'Echoes of Youth', and are forever grateful for the experiences that came with that. While writing this book was a monumental accomplishment for us, at the end of the day, we are just two teens who had an unrealistic idea and ran with it, uncertain of the outcome. We thank you immensely for taking the time to read our humble perspective. As our time together comes to an end, let us remind you, that the best stories come from within yourselves. May your own stories be filled with meaning, inspiration, and beauty. As the progress of time gracefully glides through the valleys of our lives, let life guide you to all that you wish. Be certain that the universe is conspiring to fulfill your happiness. As we leave you to ponder our message, venture into the world with open arms. Hear the echoes of your youth, and dance with the melodies of what is to come.

With gratitude and appreciation,

-Elliot Miller and Daniel Shubert.

Made in United States
Troutdale, OR
03/16/2024